Romans 9-16

The Greatest News

JOHN A. STEWART

Lamplighters International is a Christian ministry that helps individuals engage with God and His Word and equips believers to be disciple-makers.

For additional information about Lamplighters ministry resources, contact:

Lamplighters International
771 NE Harding Street, Suite 250
Minneapolis, MN USA 55413
or visit our website at
www.LamplightersUSA.org

Product Code Ro2-NK-2P

ISBN 978-1-931372-62-6

CONTENTS

How to Use This Study

WHAT IS LAMPLIGHTERS?

Lamplighters International is an evangelical Christian ministry that publishes Christ-centered, Bible-based curriculum and trains believers to be intentional disciple makers. This Bible study, comprising eight individual lessons, is a self-contained unit and an integral part of the entire discipleship ministry. When you have completed the study, you will have a much greater understanding of a portion of God's Word, with many new truths that you can apply to your life.

HOW TO STUDY A LAMPLIGHTERS LESSON

A Lamplighters study begins with prayer, your Bible, the weekly lesson, and a sincere desire to learn more about God's Word. The questions are presented in a progressive sequence as you work through the study material. You should not use Bible commentaries or other reference books (except a dictionary) until you have completed your weekly lesson and met with your weekly group. Approaching the Bible study in this way allows you to personally encounter many valuable spiritual truths from the Word of God.

To gain the most out of the Bible study, find a quiet place to complete your weekly lesson. Each lesson will take approximately 45–60 minutes to complete. You will likely spend more time on the first few lessons until you are familiar with the format, and our prayer is that each week will bring the discovery of important life principles.

The writing space within the weekly studies provides the opportunity for you to answer questions and respond to what you have learned. Putting answers in your own words, and including Scripture references where appropriate, will help you personalize and commit to memory the truths you have learned. The answers to the questions will be found in the Scripture references at the end of each question or in the passages listed at the beginning of each lesson.

If you are part of a small group, it's a good idea to record the specific dates that you'll be meeting to do the individual lessons. Record the specific dates each time the group will be meeting next to the lesson titles on the Contents page. Additional lines have been provided for you to record when you go through this same study at a later date.

The side margins in the lessons can be used for the spiritual insights you glean from other group or class members. Recording these spiritual truths will likely be a spiritual help to you and others when you go through this study again in the future.

AUDIO INTRODUCTION

A brief audio introduction is available to help you learn about the historical background of the book, gain an understanding of its theme and structure, and be introduced to some of the major truths. Audio introductions are available for all Lamplighters studies and are a great resource for the group leader; they can also be used to introduce the study to your group. To access the audio introductions, go to www.LamplightersUSA.org.

"DO YOU THINK?" QUESTIONS

Each weekly study has a few *"do you think?"* questions designed to help you to make personal applications from the biblical truths you are learning. In the first lesson the *"do you think?"* questions are placed in italic print for easy identification. If you are part of a study group, your insightful answers to these questions could be a great source of spiritual encouragement to others.

PERSONAL QUESTIONS

Occasionally you'll be asked to respond to personal questions. If you are part of a study group you may choose not to share your answers to these questions with the others. However, be sure to answer them for your own benefit because they will help you compare your present level of spiritual maturity to the biblical principles presented in the lesson.

A FINAL WORD

Throughout this study the masculine pronouns are frequently used in the generic sense to avoid awkward sentence construction. When the pronouns *he*, *him*, and *his* are used in reference to the Trinity (God the Father, Jesus Christ, and the Holy Spirit), they always refer to the masculine gender.

This Lamplighters study was written after many hours of careful preparation. It is our prayer that it will help you "… grow in the grace and knowledge of our Lord and Savior Jesus Christ. To Him be the glory both now and forever. Amen" (2 Peter 3:18).

WHAT IS AN INTENTIONAL DISCIPLESHIP BIBLE STUDY?
THE *NEXT STEP* IN BIBLE STUDY

The Lamplighters Bible study series is ideal for individual, small group, and classroom use. This Bible study is also designed for Intentional Discipleship training. An Intentional Discipleship (ID) Bible study has four key components. Individually they are not unique, but together they form the powerful core of the ID Bible study process.

1. Objective: Lamplighters is a discipleship training ministry that has a dual objective: (1) to help individuals engage with God and His Word and (2) to equip believers to be disciple-makers. The small group format provides extensive opportunity for ministry training, and it's not limited by facilities, finances, or a lack of leadership staffing.

2. Content: The Bible is the focus rather than Christian books. Answers to the study questions are included within the study guides, so the theology is in the study material, not in the leader's mind. This accomplishes two key objectives: (1) It gives the group leader confidence to lead another individual or small group without fear, and (2) it protects the small group from theological error.

3. Process: The ID Bible study process begins with an Open House, which is followed by a 6–14-week study, which is followed by a presentation of the Final Exam (see graphic on page 8). This process provides a natural environment for continuous spiritual growth and leadership development.

4. Leadership Development: As group participants grow in Christ, they naturally invite others to the groups. The leader-trainer (1) identifies and recruits new potential leaders from within the group, (2) helps them register for online discipleship training, and (3) provides in-class leadership mentoring until they are both competent and confident to lead a group according to the ID Bible study process. This leadership development process is scalable, progressive, and comprehensive.

Overview of the Leadership Training and Development Process

There are three stages of leadership training in the Intentional Discipleship process: (1) leading studies, (2) training leaders, and (3) multiplying groups (see appendix for greater detail).

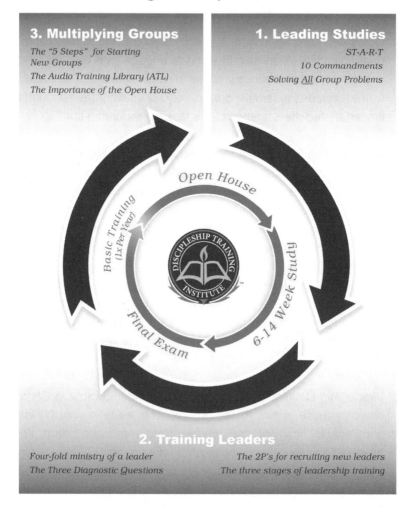

Intentional Discipleship
Training & Development Process

3. Multiplying Groups

The "5 Steps" for Starting New Groups
The Audio Training Library (ATL)
The Importance of the Open House

1. Leading Studies

ST-A-R-T
10 Commandments
Solving All Group Problems

Open House

Basic Training (1x Per Year)

6-14 Week Study

Final Exam

DISCIPLESHIP TRAINING INSTITUTE

2. Training Leaders

Four-fold ministry of a leader
The Three Diagnostic Questions

The 2P's for recruiting new leaders
The three stages of leadership training

How Can I Be Trained?

Included within this Bible study is the student workbook for Level 1 (Basic Training). Level 1 training is both free and optional. Level 1 training teaches you a simple 4-step process (ST-A-R-T) to help you prepare a life-changing Bible study and 10 proven small group leadership principles that will help your group thrive. To register for a Level 1 online training event, either as an individual or as a small group, go to www.LamplightersUSA.org/training or www.discipleUSA.org. If you have additional questions, you can also call 800-507-9516.

ONE

POTTER AND THE CLAY

Read Romans 9;
other references as given.

The first Lamplighters study on Romans (chapters 1–8) guided you through the first three major sections of the book: sin (Romans 1–3), salvation (Romans 4–5), and sanctification (Romans 6–8). You learned that all men are unrighteous in God's sight and justly under condemnation. You also learned that God declares man righteous when he trusts Jesus Christ alone for eternal life (Romans 3:21–5:21). Finally, you learned God's master plan for spiritual growth (identification, appropriation, presentation) in Romans 6–8.

As Paul's letter was being read to the Roman Christians, someone must have been thinking, "So what about the Jews? As God's chosen people, do they get a free pass? And since man is saved by faith apart from the law, does their election as God's privileged nation exclude them from the need for personal salvation?"

No explanation of the gospel is complete without answering the question of Israel's privileged relationship with God. The fourth major section of Romans (chapters 9–11) focuses on the doctrine of God's sovereignty and His divine election of national Israel.

Now ask God to bless your study of His Word and transform you into the image of His Son, Jesus Christ.

1. Paul often rejoiced during his severe personal trials (Acts 16:23–25; Philippians 1:12–18), but he also experienced

Lombardi Time Rule:

If the leader arrives early, he or she has time to pray, prepare the room, and greet others personally.

———

ADD GROUP INSIGHTS BELOW

times of great anguish and sorrow (1 Corinthians 2:1–3; Philippians 2:19).

   a. What was the specific cause of Paul's great sorrow and unceasing grief in Romans 9:1–4?

      _____

   b. What was Paul willing to do (although he was not able; the Greek imperfect tense indicates incomplete action) to save his fellow Jews?

      _____

   c. If you are a Christian, does the eternal destiny of those without Christ also cause you great sorrow and constant grief? _____

      Why? _____

      _____

      _____

2. One of the distinguishing characteristics of a mature Christian is the ability to trust God and have joy during times of testing.

   a. How could Paul instruct the Philippians to **rejoice in the Lord always. Again I will say, rejoice** (Philippians 4:4) if he wasn't able to fulfill this biblical command himself? In other words, wasn't he being hypocritical by instructing others to rejoice when he didn't do it himself at all times? Explain your answer.

      _____

      _____

      _____

      _____

      _____

b. What *do you think* Paul's example teaches you about the relationship between communicating God's command and human weakness?

_____

_____

_____

_____

Zip-It Rule:

Group members should agree to disagree, but should never be disagreable.

ADDITIONAL INSIGHTS

c. Have you ever felt that you had to be perfect before you could share God's truth with others?

_____

What is wrong with this perspective?

_____

_____

_____

_____

3. What were some of the divine privileges God gave to the nation of Israel (Romans 9:4–5)?

_____

_____

_____

_____

_____

4. The word **adoption** is used almost exclusively in the New Testament to refer to the believer's new relationship with God as a result of salvation (Romans 8:15, 23; Galatians 4:4–7). *Do you think* the phrase **to whom pertain the adoption** (Romans 9:4) means Israel had previously experienced a national or corporate salvation because of God's divine

election but now had lost their adoption/salvation due to unbelief? _____

If not, what *do you think* their adoption refers to?

_____

_____

_____

_____

_____

5. The Old Testament promises God would send a messiah who would redeem Israel and be their king (Isaiah 7:14; 9:6–7; Micah 5:2–5). Even though Israel failed to recognize Jesus Christ as the Messiah, the Word of God did not fail (Romans 9:6).

   a. What does the illustration of Isaac teach us about God's divine plan (Romans (9:6–9)?

   _____

   _____

   _____

   _____

   b. What important truth does the selection of Jacob over Esau teach about God's sovereignty (Romans 9:10–13)?

   _____

   _____

   _____

   _____

6. To some the doctrine of divine election is difficult to accept because it seems unfair and unjust. But when we realize that all men deserve God's wrath, He isn't being unjust to not save some. God is being merciful to save any.

a. What is God's answer to those who accuse Him of being unjust (Romans 9:14–18)?

_____

_____

b. What answer is given to the one who believes God is wrong to find fault with man because no one can resist His will (Romans 9:19–21)?

_____

_____

_____

Want to learn how to disciple another person, lead a life-changing Bible study or start another study? Go to www.Lamplighters USA.org/training to learn how.

ADDITIONAL INSIGHTS

7. The biblical account of Pharaoh in Egypt often strikes fear into the hearts of God's people because the Scriptures say God hardened Pharaoh's heart (Romans 9:16; Exodus 9:12; 10:27). What happened prior to the hardening of Pharaoh's heart that calms the Christian's fear about being a victim of God's pernicious and selective judgment (Exodus 8:32)?

_____

_____

_____

8. Why does God patiently endure ungodly people (**vessels of wrath**, Romans 9:22) by temporarily withholding His wrath from them (Romans 9:23)?

_____

_____

_____

9. God said He would call them **My people, who were not My people** (Romans 9:25). Whom is He referring to (1 Peter 2:9–10)?

_____

10. Some might be tempted to view Israel's inability to recognize the Messiah as a failure of God's sovereignty (Romans 9:6). What attributes of God (love, omniscience, omnipotence, mercy, faithful, righteous, just, holy, etc.) are demonstrated in His preservation of a remnant of Israel (Romans 9:27–29)?

_____

_____

_____

_____

_____

11. a. Who or what is the **stumbling stone and rock of offense** (Romans 9:33)?

_____

b. In what ways, if any, do you stumble or resist God's will for your life?

_____

_____

_____

c. If you are a Christian, how is Jesus' lordship over your life demonstrated in everyday life?

_____

_____

_____

_____

_____

Two

Beautiful Feet

Read Romans 10; other references as given.

In the first lesson you learned that God chose Israel to be the recipient of His sovereign grace. God's election of Israel bestowed numerous blessings upon the nation, but personal salvation was not one of them. The Jews, like many unsaved people today, thought righteousness was gained by fulfilling a religious code (for the Jews, it was the Law of Moses) rather than by saving faith in Jesus Christ.

In this lesson you'll learn that all people, both Jews and Gentiles, must submit to God's plan for righteousness based upon faith because Jesus Christ is the only means of salvation (Romans 10:4). You will also learn how man receives this gift of righteousness and how Christians can help others accept God's gift of salvation.

Now ask God to bless your study of His Word and transform you into the image of His Son, Jesus Christ.

1. Paul had great sorrow and unceasing grief because many of his fellow Israelites were not saved (Romans 9:2–3). List five things Paul did to reach his countrymen with the gospel— things that every Christian can do to reach others for Christ?

    1. Romans 10:1: _____

    _____

    2. Acts 14:1–3: _____

    _____

Volunteer Rule:

If the leader asks for volunteers to read, pray, and answer the questions, group members will be more inclined to invite newcomers.

———

ADD GROUP INSIGHTS BELOW

3. Acts 20:24: _____

_____

4. 1 Corinthians 9:19–23: _____

_____

5. Ephesians 6:18–20: _____

_____

2. The Jews, like many religious people today, had **a zeal for God, but not according to knowledge** (Romans 10:2). What do you think this means?

_____

_____

_____

_____

_____

3. In both the Greek and English languages the word order in a sentence can be changed to emphasize a truth (*Now* is the time to live for God; The time to live for God is *now*). In Romans 10:4, the Greek word translated **end** (Gk. *telos*; end, goal, fulfillment, conclusion) stands first in Romans 10:4, meaning greater emphasis should be placed on the word. Rewrite Romans 10:4 in your own words, using two of the four alternative words listed above for *telos*. Do your best to construct each sentence so that the word you choose for *telos* is emphasized.

1. _____

_____

2. _____

_____

4. The biblical teaching of salvation by grace through faith apart from works should not have been new or surprising to Paul's readers. Paul quotes from the Old Testament to make two key points (Romans 10:5–8). First, the person who believes he can be saved by keeping the law must obey it 100 percent of the time (Romans 10:5; James 2:10). Second, the message of salvation by faith in Moses' day was not unknown (Romans 10:8, **the word of faith is near you**).

    a. Many religious people are confused about how a person is actually saved or born again. Some believe a person is saved by joining a church, saying a prayer, being baptized, asking Jesus into their heart, or having a mystical, religious experience. What does the Bible teach about how a person is saved (Romans 10:9–10, 13; John 1:12; Acts 16:30–31)? Be as clear with your answer as possible.

        _____

        _____

        _____

        _____

        _____

    b. In his natural (unsaved) state, man doesn't possess righteousness (Jeremiah 17:9; Romans 3:10–12; Ephesians 2:1–3). What does man receive from God as a gift when he confesses Jesus as Lord and believes in his heart that God raised Him (Jesus) from the dead (Romans 10:9–10, 12)?

        _____

    c. How do the word **whoever** and the phrase **the same Lord over all is rich to all who call upon Him** influence or affect God's offer of salvation (Romans 10:11)?

        _____

59:59 Rule:

Participants appreciate when the leader starts and finishes the studies on time—all in one hour (the 59:59 rule). If the leader doesn't complete the entire lesson, the participants will be less likely to do their weekly lessons and the Bible study discussion will tend to wander.

ADDITIONAL INSIGHTS

19

5. Millions of people believe there are various ways to God. For example, New Agers believe everyone has a presence of god within them, and we are all on a journey toward divine consciousness. Others believe in sacrificing to mythical gods, engaging in a holy war (jihad), or even sacrificing to animals. What is God's answer to those who believe there are different ways to gain God's righteousness for different people (Romans 10:12–13; Acts 4:12)?

_____

_____

6. People cannot be saved or call upon Christ if they don't even understand their sinful condition and Christ's sacrifice for their sins or their need to call upon Him to save them (Romans 10:14). For people to receive the free gift of salvation, they must hear the message of salvation (Romans 10:14, **And how shall they hear without a preacher?**).

a. The phrase **And how shall they hear without a preacher?** doesn't mean that God's Word can only be proclaimed from a pulpit (Acts 8:4). List at least five additional ways or means the gospel can be proclaimed or preached to those without Christ.

1. _____

_____

2. _____

_____

3. _____

_____

4. _____

_____

5. _____

_____

6. _____

_____

35% Rule:

If the leader talks more than 35% of the time, the group members will be less likely to participate.

———

ADDITIONAL INSIGHTS

b. Some Christians believe they are exempt from the responsibility to proclaim the gospel to others because they believe they don't have the gift of evangelism, but Christ has commissioned all believers to testify for Him (John 20:21; 2 Corinthians 5:18–20). If you are a Christian, have you accepted Christ's command to tell others about their need for Christ and the good news?

Yes / No / No, but I would like to.

If you answered, "No, but I would like to," contact Lamplighters International for discipleship resources and training.

c. What are some things Christians state as the reasons why they avoid fulfilling their biblical responsibility to tell others about God's good news?

1. _____

2. _____

3. _____

4. _____

d. Of the reasons you listed above, which ones, if any, have you used to avoid sharing the gospel with others?

_____

_____

_____

_____

_____

7. Some might be tempted to believe the reason why many people are not saved is because believers have failed to share the gospel with them. According to Isaiah, why weren't

21

the Jewish people during Paul's day more willing to accept Jesus Christ (Romans 10:20–21)?

_____

_____

_____

8. God extended His love and grace to the Jewish people, but they didn't recognize Him or acknowledge His gifts (**All day long I have stretched out My hands,** Romans 10:21). In the same way God continually extends His love and grace to all people (Matthew 5:45, [God] **sends rain on the just and unjust**), even if they don't realize it or thank Him. In what ways has God extended His goodness and grace to you in the past, but you didn't realize it until later? What happened? When did you realize that God had stretched out His hand to you?

_____

_____

_____

_____

_____

_____

_____

_____

_____

THREE

THE OLIVE TREE

Read Romans 11; other references as given.

In the last lesson you learned that God was not to blame for Israel's failure to believe. Israel pursued eternal life through religious self-effort and failed (stumbled) to realize that salvation was a gift from God. The Gentiles, who did not pursue salvation by good works (obeying the law of Moses), obtained eternal life when they individually accepted Jesus Christ by faith.

One final question must be answered before entering the fifth and final section of Romans. "Has God rejected His people Israel?" (Romans 11:1). The answer to this question has profound implications for every student of the Bible. If God has rejected His people whom He foreknew and promised His faithfulness, then God's promises to Christians are also suspect. And if God has rejected Israel, then all Bible texts that speak about Israel's future must be interpreted allegorically, which rarely is a good approach to biblical interpretation.

Now ask God to bless your study of His Word and transform you into the image of Jesus Christ.

Focus Rule:

If the leader helps the group members focus on the Bible, they will gain confidence to study God's Word on their own.

ADD GROUP INSIGHTS BELOW

1. The content of Romans 11 follows the same question-and-answer format found in Romans chapter 6. Paul asks two important questions (Romans 11:1, 11) and then answers them conclusively (Romans 11:2–10, 12–36).

    a. Has God rejected Israel (**my people**) altogether? In other words, do you think national Israel has a future (Romans 11:1, 5)?

_____

_____

b. Paul lists four proofs that God did not permanently cast away (NIV: "reject") the nation of Israel (Romans 11:1–5). Please list three of them.

1. _____

_____ (v. ___)

2. _____

_____ (v. ___)

3. _____

_____ (v. ___)

2. Some Bible scholars believe God has rejected national Israel, and the church has been given the position of "spiritual Israel." According to this view (commonly known as replacement theology), there's no future for national Israel, and the church of Jesus Christ is the new **Israel of God** (Galatians 6:16). All unfulfilled promises to Israel will be eventually fulfilled by the church. Other Bible scholars believe God has temporarily set aside national Israel, but He will eventually restore the nation to a place of prominence and covenant blessing. According to this view, God will eventually fulfill every promise He originally made to national Israel.

a. What did God say to Elijah when he thought he was the only Israelite left who was still faithful to God (Romans 11:2–4)?

_____

_____

b. If the Jews didn't obtain acceptance before God based upon works, upon what basis is the remnant redeemed or saved (Romans 11:5–6)?

_____

3. There was only a remnant of Israel who believed during the days of the prophet Elijah (Romans 11:3–4) and the days of the apostle Paul (Romans 11:5). Even today there is only a remnant of the Jewish people who accept Jesus Christ as the Messiah. But this was not a mistake on God's part; this was His eternal plan. Throughout Israel's history, why hasn't there been a greater number of Israelites who accepted the Messiah (Romans 11:5–10; Romans 10:2–3, 21)?

_____

_____

_____

Drawing Rule:

To learn how to draw everyone into the group discussion without calling on anyone, go to www.Lamplighters USA.org/training.

_____

ADDITIONAL
INSIGHTS

4. The first question (Romans 11:1) could be stated as such "Hasn't God totally rejected Israel as a nation, eliminating any future relationship with Him?"

   a. Restate the question asked in Romans 11:11. Be careful to show it's distinct from the question asked in Romans 11:1.

   _____

   _____

   _____

   b. What is God's response to this second question (Romans 11:11–12)?

   _____

   _____

   c. What two things does the Bible say about how God planned to use the salvation of the Gentiles in the life of national Israel (Romans 11:12–13, 15)?

   1. _____

   _____ (v. ____)

   2. _____

   _____ (v. ____)

25

5. Paul's statement **I magnified my ministry** (Romans 11:13; NIV: "I take pride in my ministry") seems contrary to his general attitude of humility and self-effacement (1 Corinthians 3:5–7; Galatians 2:20; Philippians 2:17). Why was Paul particularly proud of when he ministered to the Gentiles (Romans 11:13–16)?

_____

_____

_____

_____

_____

6. Paul used a familiar image of a farmer or vinedresser and his vineyard to illustrate God's ongoing relationship with national Israel and Gentile believers (Romans 11:16–24). This passage, commonly referred to as the *olive tree analogy*, is rich in meaning for those who interpret it accurately. A correct interpretation of the analogy will help you understand the mystery of Israel's future and unlock many prophetic passages in the Bible. Who do you think is being referred to be the following word or phrases?

1. The **branches** who were broken off (Romans 11:17)

_____

2. The **wild olive tree** that was grafted in (Romans 11:17)

_____

3. The **root and fatness of the olive tree** (Romans 11:17)

_____

(NIV: "the nourishing sap from the olive root")

7. The olive tree analogy also includes a stern warning to **not boast against the branches** (Romans 11:18). For what two reasons should the (wild olive tree) branches not be arrogant (Romans 11:18–21).

1. _____

    _____ (v. ___)

2. _____

    _____ (v. ___)

Is your study going well? Consider starting a new group. To learn how, go to www. Lamplighters USA.org/training.

ADDITIONAL INSIGHTS

8. Do you think the passage (Romans 11:16–24) teaches that believers can lose their salvation (Romans 11:21–22, 24)? Why?

    _____

    _____

    _____

    _____

9. What do you think is the meaning of the phrase **the fullness of the Gentiles** (Romans 11:25)?

    _____

    _____

10. For approximately 4,000 years the nation of Israel has resisted the grace of God and refused to submit to God's plan of righteousness by faith. They have been preserved by God, but they have faced His chastisement and were estranged from their homeland until May, 1948. How and when will Israel be fully restored to a place of prominence in God's plan (Romans 11:28–32)?

    _____

    _____

    _____

11. The doxology (an expression of praise to God) in Romans 11:33–36 forms a beautiful conclusion to the predominantly doctrinal portion of the book (Romans chapters 1–11). Like

ADDITIONAL
INSIGHTS

a climber who has just completed his final ascent and feasts his eyes on the grandeur below, Paul reflects upon the magnificence of God's plan of redemption.

a. What words does Paul use to describe the wisdom and knowledge of God (Romans 11:33)?

_____

_____

_____

b. When was the last time you were overwhelmed with praise to God and amazed by His wonderful plan of redemption?

_____

_____

_____

_____

_____

Four

LIVING SACRIFICES

Read Romans 12;
other references as given.

The first 11 chapters of Romans are predominately theological (Gk. *theos*: God; and *logia*: study) and address the first four major sections of the book: sin (Romans 1:16–3:20), salvation (Romans 3:21–5:21), sanctification (Romans chapters 6–8), and sovereignty (Romans 9–11).

Beginning in Romans 12 the content of the letter becomes more practical in nature as we enter the final major section (service, Romans 12–16). This doesn't mean theology is devoid of practical benefit, for it's God's grace that provides the motivation and power for continuing Christian service. Tyson Edwards said, "Doctrine is the necessary foundation of duty; if the theory is not correct, the practice cannot be right. Tell me what a man believes and I will tell you what he will do."

Now ask God to bless your study of His Word and transform you into the image of Jesus Christ.

Gospel Gold
Rule:

Try to get all the answers to the questions—not just the easy ones. Go for the gold.

ADD GROUP
INSIGHTS BELOW

1. Paul urges Christians to present themselves to God as living sacrifices (Romans 12:1). The Bible lists the **mercies of God** as the reason why Christians should live dedicated Christian lives. What do you think are the **mercies of God** that should inspire believers to dedicate themselves wholeheartedly to God?

_____

_____

29

_____

_____

_____

2. The use of the word **bodies** (Romans 12:1; Gk. *somata*) is interesting. Because mere external conformity has already been condemned (Romans 2:18–29), the use of the word **body** might appear to contradict the Bible's earlier teaching.

   a. What do you think is meant by the phrase **present your bodies a living sacrifice, holy, acceptable to God**?

      _____

      _____

      _____

   b. If you are a Christian, have you ever dedicated your whole life to God for the mercies He has given you? If not, why not stop doing this Bible study right now and dedicate your life to Him right where you are?

      _____

      _____

      _____

      _____

3. When a Christian presents himself to God as a living sacrifice, it's not a heroic act; it is God's will for his or her life. The New International Version of the Bible says this is "your true and proper worship." The New King James Version of the Bible says it is **your reasonable service**.

   a. There are two other commands that require a continuing commitment from the believer (Romans 12:2). What are they?

      1. _____

Balance Rule:

To learn how to balance the group discussion, go to www.Lamplighters USA.org/training.

ADDITIONAL INSIGHTS

2. _____

b. What do you think it means to **do not be conformed to this world** (Romans 12:2; 1 John 2:15–16; James 4:4)?

_____

_____

_____

_____

_____

4 If a Christian dedicates himself to God as a living sacrifice and doesn't allow himself to be pushed into this world's mold, but allows his mind to be transformed by the word of God, he will be doing what is acceptable and well-pleasing to God (Romans 12:2).

a. What specific benefit does the Christian receive from his obedience to God (Romans 12:2)?

_____

_____

b. What do you think this means (Philippians 1:9–10)?

_____

_____

_____

_____

_____

c. Many Christians are afraid to submit themselves to God as living sacrifices because they think He might lead them into difficult situations. While it is true that God's will can involve suffering (Philippians 1:29–30), how is the will of God described (Romans 12:2)?

_____

_____

5. If celibacy is included as a spiritual gift (1 Corinthians 7:7), there are 20 spiritual gifts mentioned in the Bible (Romans 12:6–8; 1 Corinthians 7:7; 12:8–10, 28–30; Ephesians 4:11). Although some of the spiritual gifts appear to have ceased when the Scriptures were completed (1 Corinthians 13:8–10), every believer receives at least one spiritual gift at salvation (Romans 12:3, 6; 1 Corinthians12:7). While the misuse of spiritual gifts has caused great division in the church (Corinthian), the proper use of spiritual gifts can be a great asset to the work of God. Name at least four things that must be present before the exercise of spiritual gifts can benefit God's work (Romans 12:3–8, 1 Corinthians13:1–2).

1. _____

   _____ (_____)

2. _____

   _____ (_____)

3. _____

   _____ (_____)

4. _____

   _____ (_____)

6. When the Christian assumes the responsibility of fulfilling the commands God has given every believer (Romans 12:9–21), he is demonstrating willingness to be a living sacrifice for God. The first thirteen commands (Romans 12:9–13) provide instruction for believers as they interact with other

Christians. Of the commands listed in Romans 12:9–13, which two commands do you find most difficult to fulfill?

1. _____

   _____ (v. _____)

2. _____

   _____ (v. _____)

Why? _____

_____

Has your group become a "Holy huddle?" Learn how to reach out to others by taking online leadership training.

ADDITIONAL INSIGHTS

7. a. What do you think it means to **let love be without hypocrisy** (Romans 12:9)?

   _____

   _____

   b. All believers are to **abhor that which is evil** (Romans 12:9). Give two examples of how a Christian might fulfill this command to abhor what is evil.

   _____

   _____

   _____

   _____

8. Believers should not lag behind in their devotion to God (Gk. *okneros*: idle, lazy, or slack). Instead, theyshould be **fervent** (from the Gk. verb *dzeo*, to boil) in their service to the Lord (Romans 12:11). The believer who has allowed Satan to steal his spiritual intensity is a poor witness for Jesus Christ and is sinning against God. What did God tell the entire congregation at Laodicea in response to their spiritual apathy (Revelation 3:14–19)?

_____

_____

_____

_____

9. The Greek verb (*dioko*) in the phrase **given to hospitality** (Romans 12:13) means to hunt down, pursue, or run after (Luke 17:23). While we often think of practicing hospitality as having someone over to our home, how else can a Christian fulfill this important biblical responsibility?

_____

_____

_____

_____

10. If you were asked to summarize Paul's instruction to believers as they interact with fellow Christians, what two words would you use (Romans 12:9–13)?

_____

_____

_____

11. Humility is essential to the proper exercise of spiritual gifts in the church (Romans 12:3–8), the healthy relationship between believers (Romans 12:10), and the believer's relationship to the unsaved (Romans 12:16).

a. Which two commands do you find the most difficult to obey as you interact with the world (Romans 12:14–21)?

_____

_____

b. What does it mean to **have regard for good things in the sight of all men** (Romans 12:17)?

_____

_____

_____

_____

12. In one sentence, summarize Paul's instruction to the believers
at Rome regarding their relationship to those without Christ
(Romans 12:14–21).

_____

_____

_____

ADDITIONAL INSIGHTS

FIVE

THE ARMOR OF LIGHT

Read Romans 13; other references as given.

In the previous lesson you learned every Christian should present himself to God as a living sacrifice. Believers must not allow themselves to be pushed into the world's mold, and they must allow their minds to be transformed by God's Word. Only then will they be able to know God's perfect will for their lives.

In Romans 13 God's instruction continues on how to be a living sacrifice. Paul extends his teaching on the believer's responsibilities to the state (Romans 13:1–7) and summarizes all Christian conduct with one concise statement: **love your neighbor as yourself** (Romans 13:8–10). He concludes the chapter by exhorting his readers to cast off the old life of sin and darkness and fully embrace the Christ-life (**put on the Lord Jesus Christ**, Romans 13:11–14).

Now ask God to bless your study of His Word and transform you into the image of Jesus Christ.

No-Trespassing Rule:

To keep the Bible study on track, avoid talking about political parties, church denominations, and Bible translations.

———

ADD GROUP INSIGHTS BELOW

1. The Roman government was extremely corrupt at the time Paul wrote to the believers in Rome. Sexual perversion, murder of elected officials, and other forms of political intrigue and evil conduct were rampant within the Roman government. As the Roman Christians listened to Paul's letter, some must have struggled with Paul's admonition to submit to the governing authorities (Romans 13:1).

    a. Throughout history Christians have lived under both righteous and unrighteous civil governments. Why should all Christians submit to the governing authorities God has placed over them (Romans 13:1)?

_____

_____

_____

_____

b. If a Christian resists the governing authorities God has placed over him, whom or what is he really opposing (Romans 13:2)?

_____

c. List the words or phrases the Bible uses to describe the governing authorities God has ordained in our lives (Romans 13:1–6).

_____

_____

_____

_____

2. Throughout history many governing authorities have been godless, tyrannical despots. What comfort does the Bible give Christians who live under the authority of unrighteous government leaders?

   1. Psalm 2:1–5: _____

   _____

   2. Daniel 4:34–37: _____

   _____

   _____

3. There are at least four reasons Christians should submit themselves to the governing authorities God has placed over their life (Romans 13:1–5). Please list four.

1. _____

_____ (v. ___)

2. _____

_____ (v. ___)

3. _____

_____ (v. ___)

4. _____

_____ (v. ___)

If you use table tents or name tags, it will help visitors feel more comfortable and new members will be assimilated more easily into your group.

ADDITIONAL INSIGHTS

4. But for Christians the question becomes, "What if law requires a Christian to do or say something that requires me to directly violate Scripture (government-mandated abortion, ministers performing same-sex marriages, etc.)?" What did the apostles Peter and John say to the Jewish leaders who commanded them to stop speaking in the name of Jesus Christ (Acts 4:13–20)?

_____

_____

_____

5. In Exodus 1:15–20 the Pharaoh (king) of Egypt ordered two Hebrew midwives, Shiphrah and Puah, to kill all the male Jewish babies when they were born (Exodus 1:16). The midwives, however, feared God and refused to kill the male babies and even lied to Pharaoh (Exodus 1:18–19). The Bible says God was good to the midwives and established households for them (Exodus 1:21). Based upon Romans 13:1–6 and Exodus 1:15–20, do you think it was right for the midwives to disobey the governing authorities? If so, why and upon what grounds?

_____

_____

_____

6. The governing authorities include all branches of civil government that exercise some authority in a particular society. This includes elected officials and those who enforce the laws and maintain peace and order within a society.

    a. Based upon Romans 13:1; Exodus 1:15–20, and Acts 4:13–20, as well as the biblical truth that God is sovereign over all, do you think a Christian should ever disobey the governing authorities God has placed over him? If so, when?

    b. The Bible says Christians should obey the governing authorities out of fear of punishment and for conscience's sake (Romans 13:4–5)? Do you have a clear conscience regarding your relationship to the governing authorities God has placed over you (obeying the laws, paying taxes, etc.)?

7. God commands Christians to pay the taxes to support the governing officials who've dedicated their lives to the effective administration of society (Romans 12:7). But many Christians don't want their tax dollars to be used for ungodly social practices like abortion, etc. How does an understanding of the historical situation in Rome at the time of Paul's letter help Christians who wrestle with paying taxes

that are used for ungodly purposes?

_____

_____

_____

Use the side margins to write down spiritual insights from other people in your group. Add the person's name and the date to help you remember in the future.

———

ADDITIONAL INSIGHTS

8. The phrase **owe no one anything except to love one another** (Romans 12:8) has been understood as: 1. God's absolute prohibition against all forms of financial obligation (home mortgages, consumer credit, including car and student loans, etc.) or 2. God's solemn charge to insure fiscal integrity by being current on all outstanding financial obligations. Which one of these two possible interpretations do you think is correct (Exodus 22:25; Matthew 5:42; Luke 6:35)? Why?

_____

_____

_____

_____

_____

_____

9. The Bible teaches Christians to keep themselves free from all indebtedness except to love one another (Romans 13:8). Why do you think this debt to love one another can never be completely satisfied?

_____

_____

_____

10. a. Romans 13:11 says **knowing the time**. To what time do you think Paul was referring?

_____

41

_____

_____

b. What do you think is the meaning of the phrase **It is high time to awake out of sleep** (Romans 13:11)?

_____

_____

_____

11. a. Christians are to cast off **the works of darkness** (Romans 13:12). What works of darkness are all believers to cast off or discard (Romans 13:12–13)?

_____

_____

b. The Christian should put on the **armor of light** rather than living in the works of darkness, (Romans 13:11). What is this armor of light that the Christian is to put on (Romans 13:12–14)? Please be as definite with your answer as you can.

_____

_____

_____

_____

12. It is high time for Christians to awake out of sleep, cast off the works of darkness, and put on the armor of light. In what specific ways are you doing this so you can protect yourself and those you love?

_____

_____

_____

_____

Six

LIBERTY AND LOVE

Read Romans 14; other references as given.

In the previous lesson you learned that being a living sacrifice includes honoring and obeying the governing authorities God has placed over you. But the Christian's obedience to the state has a limit. If you are required by law to do something that is a direct violation of God's Word, you should obey God rather than man.

Being a living sacrifice also includes dealing righteously with other believers, especially those who are new in the faith. In Romans 14 Paul introduces two laws or spiritual principles, the law of Christian liberty and the law of love, which should govern the believer's conduct.

Now ask God to bless your study of His Word and transform you into the image of Jesus Christ.

Transformation Rule:

Seek for personal transformation, not mere information, from God's Word.

ADD GROUP INSIGHTS BELOW

1. The Old Testament law, complete with its strict dietary and feast day regulations, was given to the nation of Israel at Mount Sinai (Exodus 20:1–31:18). Christians are not under the law (Romans 6:14; 7:4, 7; 10:4), but many early Jewish believers found it difficult to discontinue adhering to the food and festival day regulations (Acts 10:9–16; Galatians 2:11–13). How does the Bible describe a Christian who still believes he or she is obligated to obey the Old Testament dietary laws (Romans 14:1)?

_____

2. The more mature Christian (**one believes he may eat all things,** Romans 14:2) understands he does not have any continuing responsibility to obey the dietary regulations of the Old Testament law.

   a. What two commands does Paul give the mature believers regarding their relationship with these weaker Christians (Romans 14:1, 3)?

      1. _____

      _____

      2. _____

      _____

   b. What instruction did Paul give to the weak believers (Romans 14:3, **him who does not eat**) who believed they were still obligated to fulfill various aspects of the Mosaic law?

      _____

      _____

      _____

3. Give three reasons believers should not judge other Christians who have different personal convictions (Romans 14:4, 8, 12)?

   1. _____

   _____ (v. ____)

   2. _____

   _____ (v. ____)

   3. _____

   _____ (v. ____)

4. A study of church history reveals a consistent inability among God's people to accept other believers who have

different personal convictions. Wearing buttons and choir robes, music styles, the use of organs in churches, bowling, drinking coffee or alcohol, attending movies, and going to restaurants on Sunday are only a small sample of the things and activities that have caused disagreement and division among God's people.

It's time to choose your next study. Turn to the back of the study guide for a list of available studies or go online for the latest studies.

ADDITIONAL INSIGHTS

a. In your opinion, what is a personal conviction, and how does it differ from a universal biblical truth—one that God expects all Christians to obey?

_____

_____

_____

_____

_____

b. Are you able to truly accept other Christians who have different personal convictions than you without judging them even if it is in your heart?

_____

_____

_____

5. a. While the law or principle of Christian liberty teaches believers not to judge one another (Romans 14:1–13), the law or principle of love teaches believers to not cause another Christian to stumble (Romans 14:14). If a believer exercises his personal liberty in Christ without considering how his actions might affect a younger Christian, what could be the result (Romans 14:15, 20)?

_____

_____

_____

_____

b. Have the actions of another Christian ever caused you to become discouraged in your walk with the Lord?

_____

_____

_____

_____

c. As a young Christian did you ever stumble over another Christian's actions and later realize that you were falsely judging the person? What did you learn from that situation?

_____

_____

_____

_____

d. Have you ever knowingly exercised your liberty in Christ and caused another (younger) believer to stumble in his or her Christian walk? If you did, what did you do to resolve the situation?

_____

_____

_____

_____

6. Try to think of a specific situation when the conduct of another believer caused you to stumble. Did you respond biblically (prayer, effective communication, etc.) or did you respond with contempt, withdrawing from that person and even gossiping to others about the problem?

_____

_____

Would you like
to learn how to
prepare a life-
changing Bible
study using a
simple 4-step
process? Contact
Lamplighters
and ask about
ST-A-R-T.

ADDITIONAL
INSIGHTS

7. What are some examples of stumbling blocks Christians place before other believers that might cause them to stumble?

1. _____

2. _____

3. _____

4. _____

5. _____

6. _____

8. a. What perspective should Christians adopt about the exercise of their personal freedom (Romans 14:21; 1 Corinthians 8:9–13)?

_____

_____

_____

_____

    b. Examine your walk with Christ. Do you have a biblical perspective about the exercise of your freedom in Christ? Why?

_____

_____

_____

_____

9. Some believers seem to pursue their freedom in Christ without regard for other believers who might be watching

ADDITIONAL
INSIGHTS

them. Instead of pursuing the unrestricted exercise of our personal freedom, what should every Christian be pursuing (Romans 14:19)?

. _____

_____

10. It is possible for Christians to become overly concerned about who might be offended by their actions. What instruction does Paul offer to avoid this trap (Romans 14:22–23)?

_____

_____

_____

11. How did this lesson change your perspective on the following:

a. Your view about personal convictions?

_____

_____

_____

_____

_____

b. The biblical admonition to walk in love with other believers?

_____

_____

_____

_____

_____

SEVEN

MARKS OF MATURITY

Read Romans 15; other references as given.

In the previous lesson Paul identified two laws or principles that should govern every believer's conduct — the law of liberty and the law of love. The law of liberty reveals the *extent* of every believer's freedom in Christ. The law of love restricts the *expression* of this freedom for the spiritual advancement of others.

Many groups study the Final Exam the week after the final lesson for three reasons: (1) someone might come to Christ, (2) believers gain assurance of salvation, (3) group members learn how to share the gospel.

In Romans 15 Paul continues to teach about the marks of spiritual maturity. A willingness to bear the spiritual weaknesses (doubts and qualms) of the spiritually immature must go beyond close interpersonal relationships. Believing Jews and Gentiles must fully embrace one another as equal members of Christ's church (Romans 15:1–13). Only then will God be truly glorified. Paul concludes the chapter by explaining why he hasn't visited them prior to this time and tells them what he would like to accomplish when he does (Romans 15:14–33).

ADD GROUP
INSIGHTS BELOW

Now ask God to bless your study of His Word and transform you into the image of Jesus Christ.

1. a. What are two characteristics of a strong Christian (Romans 15:1)?

    1. _____

    2. _____

   b. If a believer is unwilling to restrict his personal freedom in Christ through the power of the Holy Spirit for the spiritual advancement of others, do you think he should consider himself spiritually mature (Romans 15:1)? Why?

_____

_____

_____

_____

2. Mature believers should bear the doubts and qualms (uneasy feelings of doubt, fear, especially about one's own conduct) of immature Christians.

   a. Give at least three reasons why you think it's so important for mature Christians to accept younger Christians.

      1. _____

      _____

      2. _____

      _____

      3. _____

      _____

   b. If you are a Christian, do you bear the spiritual weaknesses of other believers without losing sight of Jesus Christ in your own walk with God?
   Yes / No / Sometimes /
   Yes, but I'm not sure how to do this.

   _____

   _____

   _____

   _____

   _____

3. In Romans 15:3 Paul quotes from Psalm 69:9 and applies it to Jesus, who bore the reproaches of others without losing sight of His ultimate mission. Then Paul extols (praises, commends) the value of studying the Old Testament. List several specific benefits Christians can realize from a study of the Old Testament (Romans 15:4; 1 Corinthians 10:11; 2 Timothy 3:14–17)?

    1. _____

       _____ (_____)

    2. _____

       _____ (_____)

    3. _____

       _____ (_____)

    4. _____

       _____ (_____)

4. Unity within the church of God is a dominant theme throughout the New Testament (Romans 15:5–6; 1 Corinthians 1:10; Ephesians 4:1–3; Philippians 1:27–2:4; etc.). Besides being a powerful evangelistic tool (John 13:34–35; 17:21), what other benefit is derived when God's people are united (Romans 15:6)?

    _____

    _____

    _____

5. a. The biblical teaching of unity is difficult for some believers to accept because they confuse the terms *unity* and *unanimity*. How do these two words differ in meaning?

    _____

    _____

    _____

b. Give an example of how believers within a church could have unity, but not have unanimity.

_____

_____

_____

_____

6. Some Christians' lives are characterized by self-imposed strife and conflict. Viewing themselves as God's crusaders for truth, they are often at odds with other Christians and the lone dissenting voice within a group. If they are a singular voice standing up for the truth, God bless them, but if their conflict with others is the result of spiritual arrogance, obstinacy, and self-righteousness, God help them.

a. What does God's Word say about those who cause division and conflict (Proverbs 6:16–19)?

_____

_____

b. What does Paul want God to grant the Roman (and all) believers (Romans 15:5–6)?

_____

_____

_____

c. What advice would you give another believer who constantly finds himself at odds with others for non-biblical reasons?

_____

_____

_____

_____

7. Although Christians are commanded to demonstrate graciousness toward other believers who have different personal convictions, they are commanded to admonish (Romans 15:14; Gk. *noutheto*: to admonish, warn, or correct) and even separate from certain believers at other times (Romans 16:17; 1 Corinthians 5:11–13; Titus 3:10). How does a Christian know if he should accept, admonish, or separate from another believer? (Note: the verses listed above will help you formulate your answer.)

_____

_____

_____

_____

_____

Did you know Lamplighters is more than a small group ministry? It is a discipleship training ministry that uses a small group format to train disciple-makers. If every group trained one person per study, God would use these new disciple-makers to reach more people for Christ.

ADDITIONAL INSIGHTS

8. Paul was grateful for God's mercy in his life and exceedingly thankful for the ministry the Lord had given him (Romans 15:15–21). Paul's life and ministry has been an inspiration and example to countless Christian servants throughout the ages. List at least three things Paul did as a servant of God that you could also do to be a more effective minister for God?

1. _____

   _____ (v. ____)

2. _____

   _____ (v. ____)

3. _____

   _____ (v. ____)

9. Paul said he had been hindered from visiting the Romans (Romans 15:22). When we read the word *hinder* (Gk. *egkopto*: to cut in, to hinder) in the New Testament, we often think of the work of Satan(1 Thessalonians 2:18). Who or

what hindered Paul from visiting the Romans prior to the time of his letter (Romans 15:20–21)?

_____

_____

_____

10. Paul told the Roman believers he planned to visit them after he delivered a financial gift to Jerusalem (Romans 15:25–27).

   a. What did Paul say about the financial gift and his delivery of it to the believers in Jerusalem (Romans 15:25–27)?

   _____

   _____

   _____

   _____

   b. What did Paul say about the Gentiles' financial gift to the saints in Jerusalem (Romans 15:27)?

   _____

11. What and how did Paul ask the Roman believers to pray on his behalf (Romans 15:30–32)?

_____

_____

_____

_____

EIGHT

THE HALL OF FAITH

Read Romans 16;
other references as given.

You have come to the final lesson of your study of Romans. If you have worked through the entire book, hopefully you have a better understanding of the righteousness of God. Perhaps, like Martin Luther, you now understand **the righteousness of God** (as it is used in Romans) to be that righteousness God imputes or gives man on the basis of faith in Jesus Christ alone. The Bible refers to this truth as the gospel.

The gospel was born in the heart of God (Acts 2:23), manifested in the person of Jesus Christ (1 John 3:8) and revealed by the Holy Spirit (John 16:8–11; Titus 3:5). But the gospel is not a bare theological truth; it's a soul-saving, life-redeeming, transformational reality that radically changes every life it touches.

At first glance Romans 16 appears to be a simple addendum to the book. But upon closer examination, it's the perfect conclusion to Romans because it reveals the names and testimonies of 35 people whose lives were touched by the gospel and others who are known only to God. As you read and study through Romans 16, realize that each person was originally separated from God but was rescued by the gospel and given meaning, hope, and new life in Christ by God through His grace.

Now ask God to bless your study of His Word and transform you into the image of Jesus Christ.

Final Exam:

Are you meeting next week to study the Final Exam? To learn how to present it effectively, contact Lamplighters.

ADD GROUP INSIGHTS BELOW

1. Romans 16 has often been called the layman's hall of faith because it chronicles the lives of those who received "righteousness from God." Phoebe was God's servant at the church in Cenchrea, a seaport a few miles east of Corinth. Since it was customary for letter writers to add an endorsement for the letter carrier, many Bible scholars believe Phoebe delivered Paul's letter to the Roman believers (Romans 16:1).

   a. Paul uses four words and phrases to commend Phoebe. What do the following words reveal about this remarkable woman (Romans 16:1–2)?

      1. Our sister: _____

      _____

      2. Servant of the church: _____

      _____

      3. Saint: _____

      _____

      4. Helper of many and myself: _____

      _____ .

   b. What did Paul instruct the church in Rome to do for Phoebe (Romans 16:1–2)?

      _____

      _____

2. The next members of the layman's hall of faith are Priscilla and Aquila. What does the Bible tell us about these two servants of God (Acts 18:2–3, 18, 26; Romans 16:3–5)?

   _____

   _____

   _____

   _____

Would you like to learn how to lead someone through this same study? It's not hard. Go to www.Lamplighters USA.org to register for *free* online leadership training.

ADDITIONAL INSIGHTS

3. a. What words or phrases are used to describe the people to whom Paul sends greetings (Romans 16:5–16, 21–23)? List the corresponding verse references for each commendation.

_____

_____

_____

_____

_____

    b. Now review the words and phrases you discovered in part "a" of this question. What is the most common characteristic of these little known but precious believers?

_____

    c. If you are a Christian and your name was added to the layman's hall of faith, what word or short phrase do you think would be used to describe your devotion and service to God?

_____

_____

    d. Of the words and phrases used to describe the Christians mentioned in Romans 16, which one would you most like to be used to describe you? Why?

_____

_____

e. What changes would you need to make in your life for this to happen?

_____

_____

4. Paul adds a final warning to the Roman believers to avoid certain people (Romans 16:17–18). List four characteristics of these people that all believers should avoid.

1. _____ (v. _____)

2. _____ (v. _____)

3. _____ (v. _____)

4. _____ (v. _____)

5. Paul concludes his letter to the Romans with some final greetings (Romans 16:21–23), a reminder that God's grace is with them (Romans 16:24), and a benediction (Romans 16:25–27).

a. What is God able to do for all believers (Romans 16:25)? What do you think this means?

_____

_____

_____

b. How does this happen (Romans 16:25)?

_____

_____

_____

6. The **mystery kept secret since the world began, but now made manifest** (NIV: "hidden for long ages past") is the gospel that was obscure prior to the incarnation (manifestation) of Jesus Christ (Romans 16:25–26). People were still redeemed during the Old Testament period when

they looked forward to the messiah and trusted God's promise of forgiveness by faith. What does Paul say about God and His plan of redemption (Romans 16:26–27)?

_____

_____

_____

_____

7. Final Review:

    a. What is the meaning of the phrase **the righteousness of God** as it is used in Romans?

    _____

    _____

    _____

    b. What are the five major sections or divisions of the book of Romans?
        Add the appropriate verse references if you can.

        1. _____ (_____)

        2. _____ (_____)

        3. _____ (_____)

        4. _____ (_____)

        5. _____ (_____)

8. What is God's threefold plan for spiritual growth (Romans 6:1–14, see Lamplighters Romans 1–8 study lesson # 8 for help)?

    1. _____

    2. _____

    3. _____

9. List the four most important truths you learned from your study of the book of Romans.

1. _____

_____

2. _____

_____

3. _____

_____

4. _____

_____

Leader's Guide

Lesson 1: Potter and the Clay

1. a. A great majority of the nation of Israel was not saved.
    b. He was willing to be accursed or separated from Christ (presumably for all eternity).
    c. Answers will vary, but all Christians should be greatly concerned about the eternal destiny of those without Jesus Christ. While Paul experienced great sorrow and unceasing grief, it doesn't mean that he was always downcast or somber (Philippians 2:17–18; 4:10). The eternal destiny of his fellow Israelites, however, was a constant burden on his heart. The Old Testament prophets (Isaiah, Jeremiah, Amos, et al.) were often distraught over the spiritual apathy of Israel. Christ Himself was greatly moved when He reflected on the spiritual condition of Jerusalem (Luke 13:34), and believers ought to be burdened for their families, fellow workers, and others without Christ. This concern should motivate Christians to witness and to live holy lives.

2. a. Paul was speaking the truth under the guidance and the inspiration of the Holy Spirit. The fact that he could not always rejoice made him human, not a hypocrite. Human weakness is always part of being human even if we are saved. This doesn't give believers an excuse for sinning, but it does explain the gap between what we believe and what we experience in life.
    b. Believers are perfect (positionally sanctified) in Christ, but they are not perfected (progressive sanctification). Paul wrote to the Philippians these words: **Not that I have already attained, or am already perfected: but I press on** (Philippians 3:12), and the apostle John said, "If we say we have no sin, we deceive ourselves, and the truth is not in us." (1 John 1:8). Believers should endeavor to live righteous lives, but they will never be sinless. They must comprehend this reality and accept it as a fact and press on to proclaim God's Word even if they are accused of hypocrisy.
    c. Answers will vary. No Christian is perfect. The unsaved may expect it of Christians, but God doesn't, and neither should we. All believers should strive to live wholeheartedly for God in the power of the Holy Spirit.

3. 1. God selected the Israelites to be His chosen people.
    2. God had unconditionally adopted them. They would always be His people.
    3. God manifested His glory to the nation. This means He chose them to manifest Himself to the world.
    4. God had given them specific covenants (Abrahamic, Mosaic, Davidic, New).
    5. God had given them the law. This is a reference to the law God gave to the people through Moses on Mount Sinai.
    6. God gave them the temple service. He taught them the prescribed form of true worship so that they could approach Him with confidence and find forgiveness for their sins.
    7. God gave them specific promises separate from the covenants. This included protection, provision, and various other blessings, as well promises related to judgment and restoration.

4. No. Israel's adoption refers to God's active choice of selecting national Israel to be the recipient of His sovereign grace so He might manifest His glory through them. God chose the nation of Israel to bear witness to the world (Deuteronomy 7:7). If Israel experienced a corporate or national salvation, this would be in complete violation of Scripture (John 1:12; Romans 10:9–10, 13). The reference to Israel receiving the adoption as sons reflects upon the original call of Moses to lead the Israelites out of bondage in Egypt. God refers to the people of Israel as His son (Exodus 4:22) and this is a reference to their youth, weakness, and need for protection and guidance from Jehovah. Physical descent from Abraham didn't qualify an individual to be a child of God (Romans 9:8). The Jews considered their corporate adoption—their physical descent from Abraham—to be sufficient for salvation. Paul's example of Ishmael (son of Abraham and Sarai's handmaid Hagar) proves that physical descent is insufficient for salvation, either individually or corporately. God chooses according to His own sovereign will totally apart from any human merit or superiority.

5. a. God's choice of Isaac over Ishmael demonstrates that His sovereignty is specific even to the point of choosing individual lives to fulfill His will and be the recipients of His grace. It also indicates that not all the physical descendants of Abraham are the true, spiritual seed of Abraham (believers), but it is the children of promise (in this case,

Isaac) who are accepted. It is a matter of God's sovereign choice, not an individual's physical birth, that makes someone acceptable to Him.

b. It demonstrates that there are multiple ways that God expresses His sovereignty. In the choice of Abraham, God chose him to be the father of a great nation (Abrahamic covenant). In the choice of Isaac, God exercised His sovereignty by choosing Isaac over Ishmael while the two children were still in the womb. Note: The Bible is using a familiar Hebrew way of comparison in Romans 9:13. In Hebrew, since there is no comparative as we have in English (good, better, best), the Bible often uses the "love/hate" comparative to show distinction (Luke 14:26). Although the New Testament was originally written in Greek, many of the writers were Jewish. Hebrew thoughts were conveyed by the writers without violating the doctrine of biblical inerrancy. That being said, God did not hate Esau as we would normally understand it. Paul is merely saying that God chose Isaac and extended His love toward him more than he did to Esau in this situation.

6. a. God is sovereign and He can demonstrate mercy or compassion to whomever He desires without being unjust.

b. God's selection of individuals for salvation is solely based upon His grace and mercy and is independent of their works. The clay (**the thing formed**) does not have the right to determine what kind of vessel the potter decides to make.

7. Before God hardened Pharaoh's heart, Pharaoh rejected the word of God through Moses. Pharaoh hardened his own heart, and then God hardened Pharaoh's heart. The account of Pharaoh's life parallels Romans 1:24–26.

8. God does this to make known the riches of His glory to those who have been saved (Romans 9:23).

9. Believing Gentiles.

10. Answers will vary, but should include the following:

1. His faithfulness is demonstrated by His willingness to be faithful to His promises in the face of Israel's rejection of the Messiah.

2. His holiness is demonstrated by His unwillingness to compromise the standards of righteousness and include more Israelites.

3. His justice is seen as He executed justice on His chosen people.
4. His love is seen as He preserved a remnant (Romans 9:7, 29) according to His promise.

Other answers could apply.

11. a. Jesus Christ.
    b. Answers will vary.
    c. Answers will vary.

Lesson 2: Beautiful Feet

1. 1. Romans 10:1: He allowed himself to be burdened for his fellow Jews. He prayed for their salvation.
    2. Acts 14:1–3: He witnessed to them about Christ's salvation.
    3. Acts 20:24: He did not count his own life as valuable so he could accomplish the work of testifying for the Lord to them.
    4. 1 Corinthians 9:19–23: He was willing to adapt to the person's culture as much he could without violating the gospel so others could be saved.
    5. Ephesians 6:18–20: He asked others to pray that he would boldly proclaim the gospel.

2. The Israelites were a "God-intoxicated" people, but their desire for God was more culturally sentimental than theologically solid. They thought their corporate adoption gave them personal salvation and their good works (monotheism or belief in one god, keeping the law and temple services) were acceptable to God. They had a zeal or spiritual appetite for God, but it wasn't consistent with God's Word. The Israelites' failure to understand that they were not saved merely because they were members of God's chosen people is similar to the mistake made by some churchgoers who think that they are Christians because they are members of a particular denomination.

3. 1. The conclusion of man's need for righteousness is found in Jesus Christ for everyone who believes.
    2. The complete fulfillment of the law's requirement for righteousness has been accomplished by Jesus Christ for everyone who believes in Him. Other answers could apply.

4. a. An individual is saved when he or she calls (trusts fully) upon the name of the Lord Jesus Christ and receives Him as Lord and Master. But no one calls upon the Lord as an act of intellectual pursuit. They are convicted by the Holy Spirit of their sin to the point of realizing their desperate, sinful condition before a holy God and brought to salvation by the work of the Holy Spirit (Titus 3:5).

     b. Righteousness.

     c. God's offer of salvation is available to all.

5. The Bible says there is no distinction between various ethnic groups (Jew, Gentile). There is one way to salvation, and that is through Jesus Christ who is rich to all who call upon Him for eternal life (Romans 10:12–13; Acts 4:12).

6. a. 1. Christian radio.

          2. Gospel films and movies.

          3. Christian literature (gospel tracts)

          4. Drama (Passion plays).

          5. Personal testimonies.

          6. Internet.

          Other answers could apply.

     b. Answers will vary.

     c. 1. I don't have the gift of evangelism.

          2. That's the responsibility of the pastors.

          3. I am too busy.

          4. I don't have a bold, outgoing personality.

          5. I am afraid to witness.

          6. I tried to do it and I failed.

          7. I have never been taught how to witness.

          8. I don't see other Christians doing it, so it must not be important.

          9. If God wants to save them, He is more than able to do that Himself.

          Other answers could apply.

     d. Answers will vary.

7. God extended His grace to the Israelites, but they rejected His attempts to reach them. The Bible says they were disobedient and contrary or obstinate.

8. Answers will vary.

Lesson 3: The Olive Tree

1. a. No (Romans 11:1). There has always been a remnant of Israel who has been saved (Romans 11:5).
   b. 1. Paul himself (Romans 11:1). If God had categorically rejected the nation of Israel, Paul would not be saved. Paul uses his heritage (son of Abraham and of the tribe of Benjamin; a tribe thought to hold a special position before God) as proof to show that he was part of the very core of Israel.
   2. God foreknew Israel's unbelief (Romans 11:2). Israel's unbelief didn't catch God off guard.
   3. God refused to cast off Israel when Elijah pleaded with God against Israel (Romans 11:2–4).
   4. Even in one of Israel's lowest times, God kept or reserved 7,000 people who were faithful to Him (Romans 11:4). In Paul's time there were many more than 7,000 Jewish believers (Acts. 2:1–3, 4:4).

2. a. *I have reserved for Myself seven thousand who have not bowed the knee to Baal.*
   b. God's grace.

3. Israel sought God on its own terms, which has been trying to gain salvation by keeping the law. In doing so they have been disobedient to God (Romans 10:21), and God gave them a spirit of stupor and hardened their hearts (Romans 11:8).

4. a. Answers will vary, but should be something like the following:
      If God has not totally rejected His people, could it be that Israel has sinned against God to the point (**stumbled so as to fall**) that they will never regain their privileged position before God and see the fulfillment of His promises?
   b. Certainly not. Israel is still God's chosen people and the promises He originally gave them will be fulfilled in the future.
   c. 1. God is using the salvation of the Gentiles to provoke His people to jealousy (Romans 11:11–12).

    2. Israel's future restoration (their fullness) will look like life from the dead (Romans 11:15).

5. Paul was the apostle to the Gentiles, but he did not limit his outreach to the Gentiles. He continually tried to reach the Jews and in this sense magnified his ministry. While he was being used of God to reach multitudes of Gentiles, he still experienced great sorrow and unceasing grief for Israel (Romans 9:2) and prayed for their salvation (Romans 10:1). He understood that the salvation of the Gentiles would move the Jews to jealousy and eventually cause them to return to God (Romans 11:14).

6. 1. Unbelieving Israel. The Jews who had trusted Christ and now were part of the church were still experiencing God's blessing. In the past, it was because they were part of the nation upon whom God had bestowed His blessings, but now as part of the church, they again received His blessing.
    2. Gentiles, specifically those who were saved. Notice the use of the pronoun *you* (Romans 11:17). Paul was careful to show this important distinction even though both he and the believing Gentiles were part of the church.
    3. The source of covenant blessing. The root of the olive tree was the supplier of life and abundance without which the branches could not bear fruit. National Israel had lost its supplier of covenant blessing because of unbelief, and the wild olive (Gentiles) had been grafted in. Another possible interpretation is that Abraham is the rich root of the olive tree because he was the one with whom God enacted the Abrahamic covenant. However, he was not the true root of the covenant blessing.

7. 1. God commands the Gentile church to not be arrogant (Romans 11:18, 20). That's good enough!
    2. It is the root that supports the branches, not the other way around (Romans 11:18). The branches get their life from the root. Without the root, the branches die quickly and will be removed.
    3. Christians should not be arrogant against the natural branches (national Israel). Since God did not spare them (they were broken off), then He can also remove the predominantly Gentile church from a place of corporate blessing (Romans 11). Christians should realize that their

present proximity to God's blessing is a privilege but not a right. Not only can God restore Israel to a place of covenant blessing, but He will restore them to their original place of blessing (Romans 11:23–24).

8. No. Although Paul is careful to show the distinction between believing and unbelieving Israel (**some of the branches**, Romans 11:17) and the Gentiles (pictured as **the wild olive**, Romans 11:17). Both are viewed as single entities (Romans 11:17–20, 24). Corporate covenant blessing is the subject of this parable, not individual salvation.

9. The time when the complete number of Gentiles has been saved and God's program turns back to the Jewish nation.

10. God will restore Israel to a place of covenant blessing when the total number of the Gentiles is saved (**the fullness of the Gentiles**, Romans 11:25). This will occur at an unspecified time in the future and will result in their salvation. The partial hardening that they are experiencing at this time will be removed and they will be restored to a place of spiritual privilege with God (Romans 11:26–27). Many Bible scholars believe this restoration will happen at the end of the tribulation period when Jesus Christ returns. National Israel, having experienced God's chastisement, will finally acknowledge Christ as the Messiah.

11. a. The depth of the riches, wisdom and knowledge of God, unsearchable are His judgments and ways past finding out.
    b. Answers will vary.

Lesson 4: Living Sacrifices

1. The great benefits God has given man that are recorded in Romans chapters 1–11. This includes the gift of righteousness (Romans 3:21), justification (Romans 3:28), adoption, peace (Romans 5:1), grace (Romans 5:2), atonement (Romans 5:11), eternal life (Romans 5:21), union with Christ (Romans 6:2–4), newness of life (Romans 6:4), victory over sin (Romans 6:6), freedom from condemnation (Romans 8:1), the gift of the Holy Spirit (Romans 8:2), adoption into God's family (Romans 8:15), and assurance of salvation (Romans 8:16).

2. a. To present your entire being to God as an offering, which means dedicating yourself to His purposes and willingly submitting to His will for your life. The word picture reflects the Old Testament sacrifice where an entire animal was placed upon the altar and sacrificed to God.
    b. Answers will vary.

3. a. 1. Believers should not allow themselves to be conformed to this world's goals, priorities and ideals. One Bible translation says that we are not to allow the world to push us into its mold.
        2. Christians should allow the Word of God to totally transform every aspect of their thinking so that their lives reflect the character of Jesus Christ.
    b. Christians should resist the temptation to adopt the secular mind-set of this world. A large percentage of people in any society are unsaved, and their inability to comprehend eternal realities creates a distorted cultural value system that is based on temporal goals (money, power, etc.). Success is viewed as the ability to acquire and control temporal assets (possessions, etc.) rather than being faithful to God. Christians are commanded to avoid this trap of becoming enslaved in a temporal value system that will not produce lasting satisfaction. The Christian has been given the revelation of God's Word, informing him that satisfaction will not be attained through the accumulation of possessions (Luke 12:15). He has also been given security and peace through Christ and should not allow himself to be deceived by being conformed to this world. The believer who allows himself to be conformed to this world engages in spiritual adultery (James 4:4) and allows himself to become ineffective as a witness for Jesus Christ.

4. a. He will be able to prove or determine what God's will is for his life.
    b. The Greek word for prove (*dokimadzo*) means to discern and approve after careful examination. The Christian who has dedicated his life to Christ and does not allow himself to be pushed into the world's mold, but allows his mind to be transformed into the image of Jesus Christ through personal study and regular attention to the preaching of God's Word, will be able to make accurate assessment of the value of things in life. Many believers get sidetracked because they are unable to discern between the good and the excellent things in life (Philippians

1:9–10). Paul prayed for the Philippians so that they would be able to choose the things that are excellent. Any attempt to acquire the ability to gain this kind of discernment apart from the prerequisites stated in Romans 12:1–2 will fail, and the believer will waste precious time in life retracing his steps and experiencing frustration and uncertainty about the will of God.

    c.   Good, acceptable (well-pleasing), and perfect.

5. 1.   Humility (Romans 12:3).

    2.   Understanding that God has sovereignly distributed the gifts to believers as He wills (Romans 12:3, 6). This should eliminate pride in those who have been given the more visible gifts.

    3.   A willingness to exercise the gift within the limits of faith and according to the will of the Father (Romans 12:3–8).

    4.   Love must be the foundation of the exercise of all the gifts (1 Corinthians 13:1–2).

6. Answers will vary.

7. a.   Love must be genuine and devoid of deceit. Hypocrisy (dissimulation) is the attempt to create an impression that is not real or genuine. A Christian should love others (Christians and non-Christians) sincerely and genuinely without a hint of selfishness.

    b. 1.   He should hate or abhor evil (sinful thoughts and actions, malice, bitterness, lust) in his own life.

       2.   He could take a stand in society against wickedness and evil. Other answers could apply.

8. Christ said He would spit them out of His mouth. God would remove their witness as a church (another church was told to repent or He would remove its witness or candlestick, Revelation 2:5). Christ said the church at Laodicea was deceived (Revelation 3:14–19). He said the church was spiritually impoverished (Romans 3:17). He said the church was functioning in the flesh (Romans 3:20). Note: although Revelation 3:20 is often used as a salvation verse, the immediate context is a reference to the church's unwillingness to allow Christ to have supremacy.

9. Answers will vary, but could include the following:

1. Be friendly to newcomers at work, at church, and in your neighborhood.
2. Pursue new relationships with those you know only casually by getting together with them.
3. Include new people when you get together with friends.
4. Look for ways to encourage friends and acquaintances who have become discouraged.

10. Answers will vary, but should look something like the following: Christians should be genuine followers of Christ who fervently love the truth, honor and serve other people, and give generously to the needs of others.

11. a. Answers will vary.
    b. Christians should be willing to stand up for the truth at all times. If something is wrong, it's wrong. Some Christians forfeit opportunities to be a witness for Christ by failing to testify of the truth. Their witness for Christ is often tarnished by their unwillingness to take a stand in front of unsaved friends, fellow workers, and acquaintances.

12. Answer will vary, but should look something like the following: Live a God-fearing life that honors others, seeks to walk in peace with everyone, and trusts Him to make things right when others do wrong to you.

Lesson 5: The Armor of Light

1. a. 1. They are commanded by God to do so (Romans 13:1).
      2. All civil authority is established by God (Romans 13:1). This does not mean that God endorses the sinful actions of government officials or individual legislation that they make into law.
   b. God.
   c. Governing authorities (Romans 13:1), (those) appointed by God (Romans 13:1). the authority (Romans 13:3). God's ministers (Romans 13:4, 6).

2. Psalm 2:1–5: God is sovereign over all nations, and He has contempt for their leader's wicked plans. He will speak to them in His wrath.
   Daniel 4:34–37: Nebuchadnezzar, the most powerful man on earth at that time, testified that God's kingdom is an everlasting kingdom, all the peoples of the world are as nothing in His sight, and He does whatever He

wills. No one can restrain His hand or overthrow His will or truly question what He does and decrees.

3. 1. It is God's will (Romans 13:1).
   2. If a Christian opposes civil authority, he might face judgment (Romans 13:2, imprisonment, fines, etc.).
   3. If a Christian obeys the governing authorities, he will not need to be afraid of them (Romans 13:3).
   4. If a Christian obeys the governing authorities, he will have a clear conscience (Romans 12:5; Acts 24:16; 2 Timothy1:3).

4. "Whether it is right in the sight of God to listen to you more than to God, you judge. For we cannot but speak the things which we have seen and heard."

5. Yes. The midwives were being forced to directly violate God's prohibition against murder. The midwives disobeyed the pharaoh and risked their lives to save the innocent. God honored their willingness to obey Him by establishing households for them. Their lie was a sin and a reaction to the pressure they faced. While it was not right for them to lie, it is understandable. The Lord honored them for their willingness to preserve life and in spite of their lie, not because of it.

6. a. The Bible teaches that God's people can and must disobey governing authorities when doing so would lead to a direct violation of His Word. Christians, however, are required to honor and obey the governing authorities, including the paying of taxes.
   b. Answers will vary.

7. When we understand the original historical setting and remember that Paul was writing under the inspiration of the Holy Spirit, all excuses for not paying the necessary taxes vanish. Sometimes Christians believe they are justified in withholding the payment of taxes because they do not want their tax dollars to fund governmental programs that violate the word of God. While this is honorable, it is not scriptural. Interestingly, the word render (Gk. apodidomi) means to pay back. Every citizen benefits from the amenities provided by the state (roads, hospitals, etc.). Christians are commanded to render or pay back (Gk. imperative or command) the

proportionate amount of taxes to insure the effective administration of the government.

8. # 2. God's solemn charge to insure fiscal integrity by being current on all outstanding financial obligations. While there are some Christians who maintain that a believer should never be in debt, the point Paul is making is the exact opposite. He is saying love is a debt that believers owe to their fellow man that can never be completely satisfied. Regarding the question of financial indebtedness, it is important to remember that the best interpreter of the Bible is the Bible itself. If incurring any financial obligation or indebtedness is contrary to God's will, it is hard to believe that the Lord would have said, **Give to him that asks you, and from him who wants to borrow from you, do not turn away** (Matthew 5:42). Although there are certain important distinctions between the Old Testament Mosaic covenant under which Christ spoke during the presentation of the Sermon on the Mount (Matthew 5:3–7:27) and the New Testament age of grace, the question of financial management does not seem to be one of them. The Scriptures consistently promote the principles of financial responsibility: honoring and trusting God (Romans 3:9–10); meeting our financial obligations in spite of financial hardship (Psalm 37:21), and diligent labor (Romans 12:24; 1 Thessalonians 4:11–12). It is important to note that several godly Christians (George Mueller, Hudson Taylor) believed that it was wrong to borrow at all. They were convinced (based upon Romans 13:8) that God wanted to provide all their financial needs, and God vindicated their faith by providing for their needs in a marvelous way. These men also believed that God had led them to this understanding as a personal conviction, and they did not make their perspective a test of spirituality or fellowship with other believers.

9. The Christian can only love others by allowing Christ to love them through him. Since believers are perfect in Christ (positionally sanctified) but not perfected (progressively sanctified), no believer truly loves others as Christ would love them. In this sense, all believers are still indebted to love others more and more. In this sense, love is a continuing debt that the believers will never satisfy.

10. a. The Bible teaches the imminent return of Christ (James 5:8; 2 Peter 3:1–13). Paul was referring to this event as motivation to inspire the

Roman believers to the immediate actions of submitting to government, loving their neighbors, etc.

b. Through personal spiritual renewal or awakening, a Christian gains a new awareness of his God-ordained priorities and a new fear of the consequences of spiritual apathy.

11. a. Revelry, drunkenness, lewdness, lust, strife, envy.

b. The Bible explains the armor of light in Romans 13:14. Paul says the Christian is to put on the Lord Jesus Christ. Since the admonition is something the individual does rather than something he receives, the reference here is not salvation. The Christian should fully embrace Jesus Christ, including all He is, all He commands, and all He promises. The Christian should allow Christ to work in him, through him, and for him. The Christian should give his entire life to Christ for His glory and the advancement of the cause of Christ in this world.

12. Answers will vary.

Lesson 6: Liberty and Love

1. Weak.

2. a. 1. Accept or receive them. Don't pass judgment or bring them into your assembly to argue with them.

2. Don't regard them with contempt (Romans 14:3, **despise him**). Christians should promote unity with fellow believers (Ephesians 4:1–3; Philippians 2:1–3). They should not harbor unloving or critical feelings toward other believers who have different personal convictions.

b. The weak believers were not to judge stronger believers who are exercising their personal liberty in Christ.

3. 1. We are not their masters (Romans 14:4). Even though we might think another Christian should do the things we do, Christ will keep that individual from falling if his actions are not sinful.

2. Other believers belong to God. Believers have no authority over other believers in the area of personal convictions (Romans 14:8).

3. Every believer will give account of himself to God (Romans 14:12; 2 Corinthians 5:10).

4. a. A personal conviction is something a believer feels led to do that he or she thinks is important to God and their own spiritual relationship with Him. You might say that a personal conviction is how a person applies a scriptural truth to his life. A personal conviction is often based upon a biblical truth or principle, but the actual expression of the personal conviction likely has little or no biblical support. A universal biblical truth, on the other hand, has clear and compelling scriptural support and applies to all believers.
   b. Answers will vary.

5. a. The younger Christian might stumble so badly that he may not recover (Romans 14:15). The work of God might be torn down (Romans 14:20).
   b. Answers will vary.
   c. Answers will vary.
   d. Answers will vary.

6. Answers will vary.

7. 1. Irreverent speech, including the use of profanity (including euphemisms) or sarcasm.
   2. Smoking.
   3. Drinking alcohol.
   4. Viewing television programs, movies, and videos that promote impure and immoral behavior.
   5. Overeating.
   6. Disregard for civil authority (speed laws, etc.). Other answers could apply.

8. a. A Christian should never do anything that causes another believer to stumble (Romans 14:21). Paul said he would never do anything that caused a fellow Christian to stumble even though the action was not sinful and he had liberty in Christ to do it without sinning against Christ.
   b. Answers will vary.

9. Every Christian should be seeking the things that make for peace and the building up of one another.

10. Believers should not condemn themselves for doing what God approves and the Holy Spirit does not convict them for. But Christians should be very careful that the exercise of their personal Christian liberty does not cause another Christian to stumble. This would not be an act of Christian love and could result in the destruction of another Christian's faith in God and the tearing down of the work of God. Christians should not become paranoid about trying to please everyone. If Scripture does not condemn a certain action and you have not been personally convicted that it is wrong, don't condemn yourself if you continue to do it. However, if you are still uncertain about doing a particular thing don't do it, because to do so would be sin (Romans 14:23).

11. a. Answers will vary.
    b. Answers will vary.

Lesson 7: Marks of Maturity

1. a. 1. A willingness to help younger Christians grow in Christlikeness, especially as they work through their spiritual doubts and fears.
        2. A willingness to put the spiritual advancement of others before our own personal desires. In the immediate context it includes refraining from the exercise of our personal Christian liberty when it might hinder or injure the fragile faith of a younger believer.
    b. No. A Christian's unwillingness to restrict his personal expression of his freedom in Christ for the spiritual advancement of others indicates he is more concerned about exercising his desires than about the spiritual advancement of others. This is evidence of his own spiritual immaturity and an indication that he's not mature in Christ.

2. a. 1. When a mature Christian accepts a younger Christian, it models the freedom all believers have in Christ and helps create an environment for the younger believer's spiritual growth.
        2. It is a confirming testimony or witness to God's unconditional acceptance of the young believer through the blood of Christ.

The new Christian is leaving an environment where acceptance was based upon performance (money, appearance, status, etc.), and he needs to know that acceptance in Christ is unconditional. The new Christian also may feel he's not good enough to be part of a church. If he is not accepted by older believers, he could interpret their lack of acceptance as an indication that he is not fully accepted by Christ. This could lead to legalism, which is always a detriment to spiritual growth.

3. It helps the younger Christian keep his spiritual focus on Jesus Christ, not on man's acceptance. If an older Christian is constantly telling younger Christians what to do, the young believers may take their focus off of Jesus Christ and become more concerned about pleasing other Christians. This will eventually hinder their spiritual growth.

4. Other answers could apply.

b. Answers will vary.

3. 1. Believers gain spiritual courage (perseverance and encouragement) to continue as they see how God provided for and protected His people (Romans 15:4).

2. Believers receive valuable instruction from the godly and ungodly examples in the Old Testament (1 Corinthians 10:11).

3. Believers can gain the wisdom of God that leads to a greater dedication to Christ (2 Timothy 3:15).

4. Believers can receive teaching, reproof, correction, and training in righteousness (2 Timothy 3:16). The instruction in righteousness refers to the conduct God wants every believer to manifest in his daily living that is commensurate with his standing in Christ. When the believer allows the word of God to transform his life, he will be equipped for every good work (2 Timothy 2:21).

4. It glorifies God. Harmony among God's people will bring glory to God. Because the world is filled with strife, unity between believers is a beautiful testimony of the power of Christ that brings healing and harmony to a world of chaos and confusion.

5. a. Unity is a condition of harmony, accord, oneness, or unification. For example, a literary work or artistic production can possess unity even

though it has many and complex parts. Unanimity is the quality or state of being in full agreement or unanimous.

   b. Believers could disagree about a decision that affected the church (building program, a specific ministry initiative, etc.) and even discuss it vigorously, but still be united as a body when the final decision is made. Other answers could apply.

6. a. God hates it, and it is an abomination to Him (Proverbs 6:16).

   b. Paul wanted God to grant the Roman believers a spirit of like-mindedness toward one another so that they would have a unified voice that would glorify the Father (Romans 15:5–6).

   c. Answers will vary, but should include the encouragement to examine why he or she feels the need to always be the contrary opinion and an exhortation to examine the Scriptures to learn what the Bible teaches about this important subject. The believer should be encouraged to examine himself in light of the biblical responsibility to promote unity within the body of Christ. Perhaps he does not understand his role within the body of Christ, believing he is responsible for the spiritual advancement of others. Sometimes a misguided zeal can be used by Satan to cause division among God's people. He should be encouraged to see himself as a witness (Acts 1:8), a voice (John 1:23), a servant (1 Corinthians 3:5), and an ambassador (2 Corinthians 5:20). He should also be encouraged to accept the biblical admonition that the Lord's bondservant must not be quarrelsome but gentle with those in opposition and patient when wronged (2 Timothy 2:24–26). He should be taught that love must be the foundation of all Christian service (1 Corinthians 13:1–3; Romans 12:9, 10). If this believer is willing to recognize his error, he should be encouraged to acknowledge his sin to God, asking His forgiveness and the grace to build up the body of Christ.

7. Christians should manifest an attitude of acceptance with other believers. The New Testament writer James tells us that Christians should live by the wisdom from above that is peaceable, gentle, and willing to yield (James 3:17). Paul taught the Ephesian believers that they were to preserve the unity of the Spirit in the bond of peace (Ephesians 4:3). This biblical perspective, however, must never lead to the acceptance of sin within the body of Christ (Ephesians 5:11). Jesus confronted sin in the lives of His

followers, and Paul confronted the apostle Peter for his hypocrisy and entire churches for this sin (Galatians 3:1–3; 1 Corinthians).

1. Believers should wholeheartedly accept other Christians who hold different personal convictions from themselves and allow them to grow in Christ as the Holy Spirit reveals truth to them (John 14:21).

2. Believers should admonish other believers who persist in sin and whose conduct is detrimental to the cause of Christ and harmful to the spiritual growth of other Christians. This admonition should be done only after self-examination and in a spirit of love (Galatians 6:1)

3. Believers should separate from other Christians who willfully persist in sin, but only after the biblical plan for spiritual restoration has been followed (Matthew 18:15–17).

8. 1. He wrote letters of spiritual instruction and encouragement to other believers (Romans 15:15).

2. He was careful to give God glory for everything God did through him (Romans 15:18).

3. He proclaimed the gospel wherever He could so that others would be saved (Romans 15:19–21).

9. It seems to be the leading of the Holy Spirit, who directed Paul to remain in a certain area until he had fully preached the gospel in that region. In Acts 16:6 the Bible says the Holy Spirit directed Paul and his missionary companions, even forbidding them to preach the gospel in a certain area.

10. a. 1. Paul regarded the delivery of the financial gift to the believers as a ministry or service to the saints (Romans 15:25)

2. Paul said the churches from Macedonia and Achaia were pleased to be able to give the financial gift (Romans 15:26).

3. Paul said the churches of Macedonia and Achaia were indebted to the church in Jerusalem to give the financial gift because it was the Jerusalem church (through Paul) that was responsible to deliver the gospel (spiritual things) to them. Even though Paul was the one who delivered the gospel to the churches of Macedonia and Achaia, he gave the credit to the church in Jerusalem (Romans 15:27).

4. Paul said that those who are the recipients of spiritual things (churches of Macedonia and Achaia) were under obligation to minister material things.

b. It was a debt. It was a duty.

11. 1. Paul asked the Christians to strive in prayer with him so that he would be delivered from unbelieving Jews (presumably those who thwarted his work and ministry, Romans 15:31).
2. Paul asked the Christians to strive in prayer with him so that his ministry in Jerusalem would be effective (Romans 15:31).
3. Paul asked the Christians to strive in prayer with him that he would be able to come to them with joy by the Holy Spirit. Even though Paul had a great desire to visit them, he wanted to be sure that it was God's will and in God's timing (Romans 15:32). Only then would he experience the true joy that comes from following the leading of the Holy Spirit.
4. Paul wanted the Christians to strive in prayer with him that when he visited them, it would be a time of mutual spiritual refreshment (**may be refreshed together with you**) (Romans 15:32).

Lesson 8: The Hall of Faith

1. a. 1. Our sister: Phoebe was a believer. The terms brother and sister are routinely, but not exclusively
used to refer to those within the family of God (Matthew 13:55).
2. Servant of the church in Cenchrea: Phoebe was a dedicated Christian who had identified with a local church and was a faithful servant within that congregation of believers.
3. Saint: Another name for Christian. The word saint comes from a Greek word that means "separated to." Here it refers to the theological truth that God separated Phoebe unto Himself in salvation.
4. Helper of many and myself: Phoebe was a true servant of God who ministered to many others.
b. Paul instructed the church at Rome to give her full acceptance (receive her in the Lord in a manner worthy of the saints). He also asked the church to help in any and every way she needed.

2. Aquila and his wife Priscilla were believers (Romans 16:3, **in Christ Jesus**) of Jewish descent. Aquila was born in northern Asia Minor (Pontus), but

nothing is said about Priscilla's birthplace. Aquila and his wife Priscilla apparently lived in Rome for some time, but were commanded by Roman Emperor Claudius to leave the city with all the rest of the Jews (Acts 18:2). They met Paul in Corinth where they worked together with him as tentmakers (Acts 18:3). They were hospitable believers who allowed Paul to stay with them while he was in Corinth (Acts 18:2). They were knowledgeable in the Scriptures and helped an itinerant preacher named Apollos gain a better understanding of the Scriptures (Acts 18:24–26). They had risked their lives for Paul's sake and were greatly appreciated and valued by the Gentile Churches (Acts 18:4). They allowed their home to be used as a church—a common venue for believers to meet, since there were no church buildings at that time (Romans 16:5).

3. a. Beloved (Romans 16:5). First-fruits (Romans 16:5). Fellow prisoners (Romans 16:7). Beloved in the Lord (Romans 16:8). Fellow worker in Christ (Romans 16:9). My beloved (Romans 16:9). Approved in Christ (Romans 16:10). My countrymen (Romans 16:11). Labored in the Lord (Romans 16:12). Beloved (Romans 16:12). In the Lord (Romans 16:12). Chosen in the Lord (Romans 16:13). Brethren (Romans 16:14). Saints (Romans 16:15). Fellow worker (Romans 16:21). Countrymen (Romans 16:21). Brother (Romans 16:23).
   b. Beloved in the Lord, brethren, fellow workers.
   c. Answers will vary.
   d. Answers will vary.
   e. Answers will vary.

4. 1. They cause divisions and offenses (Romans 16:17).
   2. They don't live according to God's Word (contrary to the doctrine, Romans 16:18).
   3. They serve themselves (their own belly) rather than the Lord Jesus (Romans 16:17). Perhaps the reference here to their own bellies refers to indulgent physical desires with special reference to gluttony and drunkenness (Romans 16:18).
   4. They are smooth-talkers who use flattery to their advantage and deceive others (Romans 16:18).

5. a. God is able to establish all believers in the Lord, which means to bring them to spiritual maturity. He does this through the preaching of the

gospel. Here the reference to the gospel is not restricted to the plan of salvation. It refers to the entirety of God's message as revealed in the New Testament (the mystery kept secret since the world began).

b. God establishes His people in the faith through the proclamation of His Word. This occurs when the Word of God is preached faithfully and when His people accept their rightful role as witnesses and ambassadors of the truth.

6. The everlasting God revealed his plan of redemption (gospel) in the Scriptures. This plan was revealed to all nations, not just the Jews, so that obedience to His will could be accomplished (Romans 16:26). This plan was revealed by God who alone is wise and for His glory as He revealed it through Jesus Christ who exists forever.

7. a. The righteousness that God offers to man as a voluntary expression of His sovereign grace whereby man can be declared righteous. This righteousness is offered by God freely to man apart from work and is accepted by faith alone through grace alone.

   b. 1. Sin (Romans 1:1–3:20)
      2. Salvation (Romans 3:21–4:25)
      3. Sanctification (Romans chapters 6–8)
      4. Sovereignty (Romans chapters 9–11)
      5. Service (Romans chapters 12–16)

8. Identification. Appropriation. Presentation.

9. Answers will vary.

ADDITIONAL INSIGHTS

FINAL EXAM

Every person will eventually stand before God in judgment—the final exam. The Bible says, *And it is appointed for men to die once, but after this the judgment* (Hebrews 9:27).

May I ask you a question? *If you died today, do you know for certain you would go to heaven?* I did not ask if you're religious or a church member, nor did I ask if you've had some encounter with God—a meaningful spiritual experience. I didn't even ask if you believe in God or angels or if you're trying to live a good life. The question I *am* asking is this: *If you died today, do you know for certain you would go to heaven?*

When you die, you will stand alone before God in judgment. You'll either be saved for all eternity, or you will be separated from God for all eternity in what the Bible calls the lake of fire (Romans 14:12; Revelation 20:11–15). Tragically, many religious people who believe in God are not going to be accepted by Him when they die.

Many will say to Me in that day, "Lord, Lord, have we not prophesied in Your name, cast out demons in Your name, and done many wonders in Your name?" And then I will declare to them, "I never knew you; depart from Me, you who practice lawlessness!" (Matthew 7:22–23)

God loves you and wants you to go to heaven (John 3:16; 2 Peter 3:9). If you are not sure where you'll spend eternity, you are not prepared to meet God. God wants you to know for certain that you will go to heaven.

Behold, now is the accepted time; behold, now is the day of salvation. (2 Corinthians 6:2)

The words *behold* and *now* are repeated because God wants you to know that you can be saved today. You do not need to hear those terrible words, *Depart from Me ....* Isn't that great news?

Jesus himself said, *You must be born again* (John 3:7). These aren't the words of a pastor, a church, or a particular denomination. They're the words of Jesus Christ himself. You *must* be born again (saved from eternal damnation) before you die; otherwise, it will be too late when you die! You can know for certain today that God will accept you into heaven when you die.

These things I have written to you who believe in the name of the Son of God, that you may know that you have eternal life.

(1 John 5:13)

The phrase **you may know** means that you can know for certain before you die that you will go to heaven. To be born again, you must understand and accept four essential spiritual truths. These truths are right from the Bible, so you know you can trust them—they are not man-made religious traditions. Now, let's consider these four essential spiritual truths.

Essential Spiritual Truth

#1

The Bible teaches that you are a sinner and separated from God.

No one is righteous in God's eyes. To be righteous means to be totally without sin, not even a single act.

There is none righteous, no, not one;
There is none who understands;
There is none who seeks after God.
They have all turned aside;
They have together become unprofitable;
There is none who does good, no, not one.
(Romans 3:10–12)

...for all have sinned and fall short of the glory of God.
(Romans 3:23)

Look at the words God uses to show that all men are sinners—**none, not one, all turned aside, not one**. God is making a point: all of us are sinners. No one is good (perfectly without sin) in His sight. The reason is sin.

Have you ever lied, lusted, hated someone, stolen anything, or taken God's name in vain, even once? These are all sins.

Are you willing to admit to God that you are a sinner? If so, then tell Him right now you have sinned. You can say the words in your heart or aloud—it doesn't matter which—but be honest with God. Now check the box if you have just admitted you are a sinner.

☐ God, I admit I am a sinner in Your eyes.

Spiritual Death

Eternal Life

Now, let's look at the second essential spiritual truth.

Essential Spiritual Truth

#2

The Bible teaches that you cannot save yourself or earn your way to heaven.

Man's sin is a very serious problem in the eyes of God. Your sin separates you from God, both now and for all eternity—unless you are born again.

For the wages of sin is death.
(Romans 6:23)

And you He made alive, who were dead in trespasses and sins.
(Ephesians 2:1)

Wages are a payment a person earns by what he or she has done. Your sin has earned you the wages of death, which means separation from God. If you die never having been born again, you will be separated from God after death.

You cannot save yourself or purchase your entrance into heaven. The Bible says that man is **not redeemed with corruptible things, like silver or gold** (1 Peter 1:18). If you owned all the money in the world, you still could not buy your entrance into heaven. Neither can you buy your way into heaven with good works.

For by grace you have been saved through faith, and that not of yourselves; it is the gift of God, not of works, lest anyone should boast. (Ephesians 2:8–9)

The Bible says salvation is **not of yourselves**. It is **not of works, lest anyone should boast**. Salvation from eternal judgment cannot be earned by doing good works; it is a gift of God. There is nothing you can do to purchase your way into heaven because you are already unrighteous in God's eyes.

If you understand you cannot save yourself, then tell God right now that you are a sinner, separated from Him, and you cannot save yourself. Check the box below if you have just done that.

☐ God, I admit that I am separated from You because of my sin. I realize that I cannot save myself.

Now, let's look at the third essential spiritual truth.

Essential Spiritual Truth

#3

The Bible teaches that Jesus Christ died on the cross to pay the complete penalty for your sin and to purchase a place in heaven for you.

Jesus Christ, the sinless Son of God, lived a perfect life, died on the cross, and rose from the dead to pay the penalty for your sin and purchase a place in heaven for you. He died on the cross on your behalf, in your place, as your substitute, so you do not have to go to hell. Jesus Christ is the only acceptable substitute for your sin.

> *For He [God, the Father] made Him [Jesus] who knew [committed] no sin to be sin for us, that we might become the righteousness of God in Him.*
> (2 Corinthians 5:21)

> *I [Jesus] am the way, the truth, and the life. No one comes to the Father except through Me.*
> (John 14:6)

Nor is there salvation in any other, for there is no other name under heaven given among men by which we must be saved.
(Acts 4:12)

Jesus Christ is your only hope and means of salvation. Because you are a sinner, you cannot pay for your sins, but Jesus paid the penalty for your sins by dying on the cross in your place. Friend, there is salvation in no one else—not angels, not some religious leader, not even your religious good works. No religious act such as baptism, confirmation, or joining a church can save you. There is no other way, no other name that can save you. Only Jesus Christ can save you. You must be saved by accepting Jesus Christ's substitutionary sacrifice for your sins, or you will be lost forever.

Do you see clearly that Jesus Christ is the only way to God in heaven? If you understand this truth, tell God that you understand, and check the box below.

☐ God, I understand that Jesus Christ died to pay the penalty for my sin. I understand that His death on the cross was the only acceptable sacrifice for my sin.

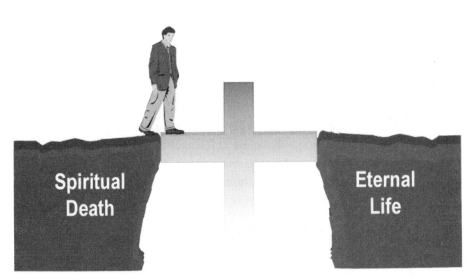

Essential Spiritual Truth

#4

By faith, you must trust in Jesus Christ alone for eternal life and call upon Him to be your Savior and Lord.

Many religious people admit they have sinned. They believe Jesus Christ died for the sins of the world, but they are not saved. Why? Thousands of moral, religious people have never completely placed their faith in Jesus Christ *alone* for eternal life. They think they must believe in Jesus Christ as a real person and do good works to earn their way to heaven. They are not trusting Jesus Christ alone. To be saved, you must trust in Jesus Christ *alone* for eternal life. Look what the Bible teaches about trusting Jesus Christ alone for salvation.

Believe on the Lord Jesus Christ, and you will be saved.
(Acts 16:31)

...that if you confess with your mouth the Lord Jesus and believe in your heart that God has raised Him from the dead, you will be saved. For with the heart one believes unto righteousness, and with the mouth confession is made unto salvation.... For there is no distinction between Jew and Greek, for the same Lord over all is rich to all who call upon Him. For "whoever calls on the name of the Lord shall be saved.
(Romans 10:9–10, 12–13)

Do you see what God is saying? To be saved or born again, you must trust Jesus Christ *alone* for eternal life. Jesus Christ paid for your complete salvation. Jesus said, **It is finished!** (John 19:30). Jesus paid for your salvation completely when He shed His blood on the cross for your sin.

If you believe that God resurrected Jesus Christ (proving God's acceptance of Jesus as a worthy sacrifice for man's sin) and you are willing to confess Jesus Christ as your Savior and Lord (master of your life), you will be saved.

Friend, right now God is offering you the greatest gift in the world. God wants to give you the *gift* of eternal life, the *gift* of His complete forgiveness for all your sins, and the *gift* of His unconditional acceptance into heaven when you die. Will you accept His free gift now, right where you are?

Are you unsure how to receive the gift of eternal life? Let me help you. Do you remember that I said you needed to understand and accept four essential spiritual truths? First, you admitted you are a sinner. Second, you admitted you were separated from God because of your sin and you could not save yourself. Third, you realized that Jesus Christ is the only way to heaven—no other name can save you.

Now, you must trust that Jesus Christ died once and for all to save your lost soul. Just take God at His word—He will not lie to you! This is the kind of simple faith you need to be saved. If you would like to be saved right now, right where you are, offer this prayer of simple faith to God. Remember, the words must come from your heart.

God, I am a sinner and deserve to go to hell. Thank You, Jesus, for dying on the cross for me and for purchasing a place in heaven for me. I believe You are the Son of God and You are able to save me right now. Please forgive me for my sin and take me to heaven when I die. I invite You into my life as Savior and Lord, and I trust You alone for eternal life. Thank You for giving me the gift of eternal life. Amen.

If, in the best way you know how, you trusted Jesus Christ alone to save you, then God just saved you. He said in His Holy Word, *But as many as received Him, to them He gave the right to become the children of God* (John 1:12). It's that simple. God just gave you the gift of eternal life by faith. You have just been born again, according to the Bible.

You will not come into eternal judgment, and you will not perish in the lake of fire—you are saved forever! Read this verse carefully and let it sink into your heart.

> ***Most assuredly, I say to you, he who hears My word and believes in Him who sent Me has everlasting life, and shall not come into judgment, but has passed from death into life.***
> (John 5:24)

Now, let me ask you a few more questions.

According to God's holy Word (John 5:24), not your feelings, what kind of life did God just give you? _____

What two words did God say at the beginning of the verse to assure you that He is not lying to you? _____   _____

Are you going to come into eternal judgment? ☐ YES   ☐ NO

Have you passed from spiritual death into life? ☐ YES   ☐ NO

Friend, you've just been born again. You just became a child of God.

To help you grow in your new Christian life, we would like to send you some Bible study materials. To receive these helpful materials free of charge, e-mail your request to **info@LamplightersUSA.org.**

Spiritual Death

Eternal Life

Appendix

Level 1 (Basic Training)
Student Workbook

To begin, familiarize yourself with the Lamplighters' *Leadership Training and Development Process* (see graphic on page 96). Notice there are two circles: a smaller, inner circle and a larger, outer circle. The inner circle shows the sequence of weekly meetings beginning with an Open House, followed by an 8–14 week study, and concluding with a clear presentation of the gospel (Final Exam). The outer circle shows the sequence of the Intentional Discipleship training process (Leading Studies, Training Leaders, Multiplying Groups). As participants are transformed by God's Word, they're invited into a discipleship training process that equips them in every aspect of the intentional disciple-making ministry.

The Level 1 training (Basic Training) is *free*, and the training focuses on two key aspects of the training: 1) how to prepare a life-changing Bible study (ST-A-R-T) and 2) how to lead a life-changing Bible study (10 commandments). The training takes approximately 60 minutes to complete, and you complete it as an individual or collectively as a small group (preferred method) by inserting an extra week between the Final Exam and the Open House.

To begin your training, go to www.LamplightersUSA.org to register yourself or your group. A Lamplighters' Certified Trainer will guide you through the entire Level 1 training process. After you have completed the training, you can review as many times as you like.

When you have completed the Level 1 training, please consider completing the Level 2 (Advanced) training. Level 2 training will equip you to reach more people for Christ by learning how to train new leaders and by showing you how to multiply groups. You can register for additional training at www. LamplightersUSA.org.

Intentional Discipleship
Training & Development Process

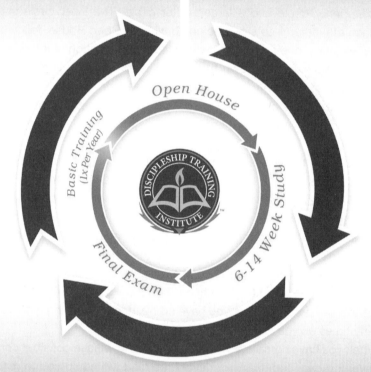

3. Multiplying Groups

The "5 Steps" for Starting
New Groups
The Audio Training Library (ATL)
The Importance of the Open House

1. Leading Studies

ST-A-R-T
10 Commandments
Solving All Group Problems

Open House

Basic Training
(1x Per Year)

6-14 Week Study

Final Exam

DISCIPLESHIP TRAINING INSTITUTE

2. Training Leaders

Four-fold ministry of a leader
The Three Diagnostic Questions

The 2P's for recruiting new leaders
The three stages of leadership training

How to Prepare a
Life-Changing Bible Study
ST-A-R-T

Step 1: _____ and _____.

Pray specifically for the group members and yourself as you study God's Word. Ask God (_____) to give each group member a rich time of personal Bible study, and thank (_____) God for giving you a desire to invest in the spiritual advancement of each other.

Step 2: _____ the _____.

Answer the questions in the weekly lessons without looking at the

_____ _____.

Step 3: _____ and _____.

Review the Leader's Guide, and _____ every truth you missed when you originally did your lesson. Record the answers you missed with a

_____ _____ so you'll know what you missed.

Step 4: _____ _____.

Calculate the specific amount of time _____ _____ to spend on each question and write the start time next to each one in the

_____ using a _____.

How to Lead a Life-Changing Bible Study

10 COMMANDMENTS

1	2	3
4	5	6
7	8	9
	10	

Lamplighters' 10 Commandments are proven small group leadership principles that have been used successfully to train hundreds of believers to lead life-changing, intentional discipleship Bible studies.

Essential Principles for Leading Intentional Discipleship Bible Studies

1. The 1st Commandment: The _____ Rule.
   The Leader-Trainer should be in the room _____ minutes before the class begins.

2. The 2nd Commandment: The _____-_____ Rule.
   Train the group that it is okay to _____, but they should never be
   _____.

3. The 3rd Commandment: The _____ Rule.
   _____, _____, _____ ask for
   _____ to _____ the _____, _____, and _____
   the questions. The Leader-Trainer, however, should always _____ the
   questions to control the _____ of the study.

4. The 4th Commandment: The _____:_____ Rule.
   _____ the Bible study on time and _____ the study on time
   _____ _____. No exceptions!

5. The 5th Commandment: The _____ Rule.
   Train the group participants to _____ on God's Word for answers
   to life's questions.

1	2	3
4 **59:59**	5	6
7	8	9
	10	

6. The 6th Commandment: The _____ Rule.

   Deliberately and progressively _____ _____ participants into the group discussion over a period of time.

7. The 7th Commandment: The _____ _____ Rule.

   _____ the participants to get _____ the answers to the questions, not just _____ or _____ ones.

8. The 8th Commandment: The _____ Rule.

   _____ the group discussion so you _____ the lesson _____ _____ and give each question _____ _____.

9. The 9th Commandment: The _____-_____ Rule.

   Don't let the group members talk about _____ _____, _____ _____, or _____ _____.

10. The 10th Commandment: The _____ Rule.

   _____ God to change lives, including _____.

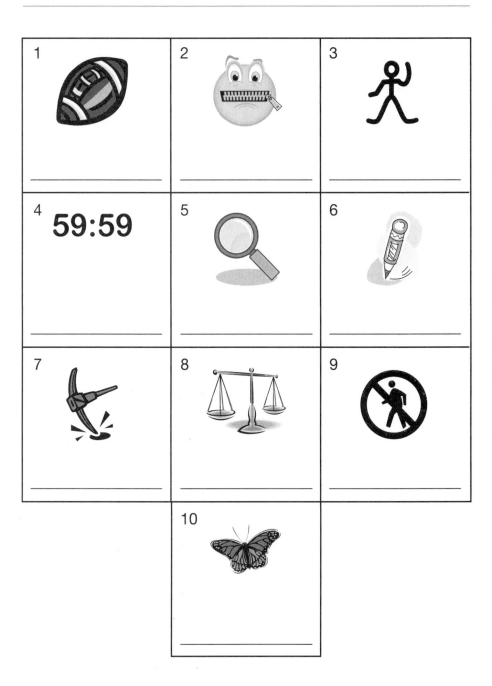

Choose your next study from any of the following titles:

- Joshua 1-9
- Joshua 10-24
- Judges 1-10
- Judges 11-21
- Ruth/Esther
- Jonah/Habakkuk
- Nehemiah
- Proverbs 1-9
- Proverbs 10-31
- Ecclesiastes
- John 1-11
- John 12-21
- Acts 1-12
- Acts 13-28

- Romans 1-8
- Romans 9-16
- Galatians
- Ephesians
- Philippians
- Colossians
- 1 & 2 Thessalonians
- 1 Timothy
- 2 Timothy
- Titus/Philemon
- Hebrews
- James
- 1 Peter
- 2 Peter/Jude

Additional Bible studies and sample lessons are available online.

For audio introductions on all Bible studies, visit us online at www.Lamplightersusa.org.

Looking to begin a new group?
The Lamplighters Starter Kit includes:

- 8 James Bible Study Guides (students purchase their own books)
- 25 Welcome Booklets
- 25 Table Tents
- 25 Bible Book Locator Bookmarks
- 50 Final Exam Tracts
- 50 Invitation Cards

For a current listing of live and online discipleship training events, or to register for discipleship training, go to www.LamplightersUSA.org/training.

Become a Certified Disciple-Maker

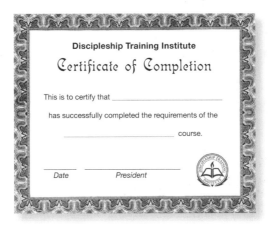

Discipleship Training Institute

Certificate of Completion

This is to certify that _____

has successfully completed the requirements of the

_____ course.

_____ _____
Date   President

Training Courses Available:

- Leader-Trainer
- Discipleship Coach
- Discipleship Director

Contact the Discipleship Training Institute for more information (800-507-9516).

The Discipleship Training Institute is a ministry of Lamplighters International.